医学SCI论文撰写与发表

（第二版）

English for Writing Medical Research Papers

Second Edition

编 著 卢凤香 郭 晶 陶 鑫

华 瑶 杨 波 李国英

中国协和医科大学出版社

北 京

图书在版编目（CIP）数据

医学 SCI 论文撰写与发表 / 卢凤香等编著 .—2 版 .—北京：中国协和医科大学出版社，2022.8

ISBN 978-7-5679-2020-0

Ⅰ.①医… Ⅱ.①卢… Ⅲ.①医学－论文－写作 Ⅳ.①H152.2

中国版本图书馆 CIP 数据核字（2022）第 125427 号

医学 SCI 论文撰写与发表（第二版）

编　　著：卢凤香　郭　晶　陶　鑫　华　瑶　杨　波　李国英
责任编辑：李书鹏
封面设计：许晓晨
责任校对：张　麓
责任印制：张　岱

出版发行：中国协和医科大学出版社
（北京市东城区东单三条 9 号　邮编 100730　电话 010－65260431）
网　　址：www.pumcp.com
经　　销：新华书店总店北京发行所
印　　刷：小森印刷（北京）有限公司

开　　本：787mm×1092mm　1/16
印　　张：13.5
字　　数：270 千字
版　　次：2022 年 8 月第 2 版
印　　次：2024 年 1 月第 2 次印刷
定　　价：68.00 元

ISBN 978-7-5679-2020-0

再版前言

《医学 SCI 论文撰写与发表》自 2016 年 1 月出版以来，深受医学院校师生、医学科技人员以及医务工作者们的好评，第一版已印刷 6 次。同时，本书作为提高医学生写作能力的专业教材被广泛应用于多家医学院校，极大地促进了全国医学院校医学英语写作课程的建设与发展。

本书第一版重点关注了医学生、医学科技人员以及医务工作者撰写医学学术论文时常遇到的英语语言表达适切问题以及论文撰写完成后向国际期刊投稿发表过程中与编审的有效沟通问题。但随着数字资源建设的不断发展以及新的线上线下混合式教学模式的不断迭代，针对提高医学生医学写作能力的专业教材需要紧跟时代发展步伐，回应时代发展对专业写作能力教材的新需求，满足读者基于慕课资源进行自主学习的要求，为读者提供自主学习的资源和途径，因此编写组启动了第二版的修订工作。

本次修订沿用了第一版的编写框架，分别是“语言写作基础”和“学术论文构成”两部分。第一部分在原有内容基础上补充了实操练习，第二部分增加了大量真实的期刊案例赏析和练习。本版修订特色具体体现在以下三个方面。

一是构建了纸质教材和数字教材相结合的立体资源链。

线上线下混合式教学模式的开展需要高质量的线上资源支撑。以本书为基础的“医学 SCI 论文写作”慕课已于 2020 年 10 月上线，目前已完成 5 轮课程，选课人数近 2 万。修订后的纸质版教材从知识体系、组织架构和选材内容上对接慕课课程内容，与慕课资源配套共同构建起立体化教学资源链，服务于医学院校线上线下混合式教学模式的开展以及读者自主学习与应用。

二是增加了供课堂教学使用及读者可学习、可赏析的期刊写作范例。

本版第二部分增加了案例赏析（Case Analysis）。案例选自临床期刊 *The Lancet*，*The New England Journal of Medicine*，*Journal of American Medical Association* 和 *British Medical Journal*。对选取的文章，分别针对标题、摘要、引言、方法、结果以及讨论（结论）进行功能、结构、语言等多层次分析，鉴赏重点句型的用词与结构，帮助读者依照范文完成论文写作训练。

三是补充了从理论到实践应用的大量实操习题。

为了便于读者在学习理论和赏析范文后开展实操训练，本次修订还增加了思考练习题，练习内容丰富，形式多样，既涵盖知识型，也包括应用型，方便读者随时对自主学习情况进行自我评价。习题均在附录部分提供参考答案，方便读者自测自评。为便于读者查阅本书中所选案例的全文，附录中提供了具体文献搜索信息。

本次修订由首都医科大学卢凤香、郭晶、陶鑫、华瑶、杨波和李国英六位教师共同完成。此次修订的文稿中有很多医学专家学者们投稿、交流的原文，在此对这些专家学者，特别是首都医科大学基础医学院曲爱娟教授，在我们修订过程中给予的支持表示衷心感谢。此外，本书选取了上述提到的四种英文期刊上的文章，没有这些文章，也就没有本书中案例的分析和启迪，在此向这些案例文章的作者们表示诚挚的谢意。

虽然本书作者在修订中努力做到严谨、认真，但囿于能力所限，特别是医学专业知识薄弱，书中可能会有很多不足，甚至谬误，还请各位读者批评指正。

卢凤香

2022 年 8 月于首都医科大学

前 言

对全世界的学者来说，要想使自己的研究成果被更多人了解和接受，用英语撰写论文并在国际性学术期刊上发表已经成为一种势在必行的选择。近年来，医学院校的师生、医学研究机构的科研人员和医务工作者用英文撰写和发表科研论文已成常态。SCI 论文的结构布局、论证的逻辑性以及语言表达方式上都有其特定的要求，但由于英语作为一种外语，虽然论文作者们大都有过十多年，乃至更长时间的英语学习经历，但用规范的学术英语语言进行写作表达的能力依然欠佳。虽然其论文的观点和数据都很好，但往往由于英语语言表达不到位，甚至表达错误，导致论文不被接受和发表，这实在是一种遗憾。

本书旨在通过系统、细致地介绍学术英语语言特点，为撰写医学论文的学者在各类 SCI 期刊上发表更多、更好的学术文章提供实质性的语言帮助。本书由两大部分组成，第一部分为 SCI 学术论文词汇、句子、段落的写作风格，包括选词如何做到清晰、准确和简洁；句子表达如何恰如其分；段落如何具有逻辑性。第二部分为 SCI 学术论文中摘要、标题、引言、方法、结果、讨论等各部分的功能与结构以及语言组织的特点。除此之外，本书还包括了 SCI 论文撰写过程中标点符号以及参考文献撰写中的注意事项。每一章节还提供必要的练习材料，以加强读者对本章内容的掌握和吸收。

全书共 14 章，英语语言易懂，所举范例易于理解和模仿，特别是本书采用了英汉两种语言表达形式，对撰写论文中容易出错的地方以中文旁批的形式给与进一步的阐述和注释，便于读者理解和准确把握。适用对象为医（药）学院校、生物医学科研单位、各级医疗机构医、教、研人员及研究生、医学生。

James Boulton　卢凤香　郭　晶

2015 年 7 月于首都医科大学

Contents

Part I

Academic Writing: Form, Function and Style

Style is achieved in writing just as it is achieved in fashion, not by changing the function of the material in question, but by changing the form. Any number of different coats may keep a person warm on a cold day, but each coat will give a different impression of that person. Much in the same way, any number of forms may be used to express the same idea in writing, but the different forms each create a different style and a different impression. Just as it would be difficult to be admitted into an important formal function in shorts, sandals and a T-shirt, it is difficult to be admitted into the academic community without mastering an academic style of writing.

An academic writing style is achieved through techniques applied to different levels of text analysis from the basic rules for punctuation all the way to methods for creating a unified story out of a complex relationship of concepts (Gee, 1985). **Part I** of this book begins with the mechanics of writing in an academic style and then gradually moves to larger and more comprehensive levels of discourse.

Chapter One Writing Mechanics

The technical aspects of writing, including punctuation, capitalization and spelling, provide the framework for the text. The framework should be in the background, unnoticed; if it is noticed, it usually means that something is wrong. Because of this, any errors or nonstandard applications of punctuation, capitalization and spelling will interrupt the flow of the narrative, and should be carefully searched for and eliminated.

Although these types of mistakes do not usually affect the content, they do affect the way that the reader will respond to the writing. Mistakes in punctuation, spacing and spelling give the reader an impression of a careless writer. Although this may not be the case, the impression is still conveyed.

1. The Forms and Functions of Common Punctuation

1.1 Period .

Periods are placed at the end of a sentence. No space is placed before a period, and one space separates a period from the following sentence (Example 1).

Example 1

Punctuation is used to separate and organize ideas within and between sentences. Reading becomes difficult when a text has been punctuated improperly.

Periods are placed after numbers or letters used to organize a list. No space is placed between the number and the period, and one space is placed after the period (Example 2).

Example 2

1. Form
2. Function
3. Style

1.2 Comma ,

Commas have several related functions in writing. A comma is used to emphasize a separation between phrases and clauses (Example 3) and to set apart an unrestrictive phrase or clause (Example 4) (Strunk, 2006). Commas are also used to separate the elements in a list when the list has more than two items (Example 5). A comma cannot be used to connect two main clauses (Example 6). A comma has no space before it and one space after it (Example 3-6).

Example 3

To emphasize a phrase, a comma can be used.

Example 4

The comma, a common punctuation mark, can sometimes be overused.

Example 5

Commas, periods and semicolons are the most common punctuation marks.

Example 6

Incorrect

Commas are not able to link two main clauses, they do not have this power.

Correct

Commas are not able to link two main clauses. They do not have this power.

1.3 Semicolon ;

A semicolon is used to merge two sentences into one, in order to emphasize the connection between the two sentences. Unlike a comma, a semicolon can be used to connect two main clauses (Example 7). A semicolon has no space before it and one space after it (Example 7).

Example 7

Semicolons are able to link two main clauses; they have this power.

1.4 Dash —

A dash is used to separate nonrestrictive information within a sentence (Example 7). It falls between commas and parentheses in regards to the strength of separation. A dash has no space before or after it (Example 8).

Example 8

A dash—but not a comma—creates a strong separation of ideas within a sentence.

1.5 Hyphen -

A hyphen is used to clarify ambiguity caused by multiple modifiers. Adjectives and adverbs are linked to other modifiers with a hyphen if there is a possibility that the link could be misinterpreted. This possibility sometimes occurs when a series of modifiers precedes a noun (Example 9).

Example 9

Stem-cell graft

1.6 Parentheses ( )

Parentheses are also used to isolate information within a sentence. The sentence must be understandable if a reader ignores the information in the parentheses. In research papers, parentheses are important ways to include details without interrupting the flow of ideas. The types of information found within parentheses include citations, figure and table numbers, weights, doses, sample sizes, raw data and manufacturers' names (Example 10). One space precedes the first parentheses. No space is placed between the first or second parentheses and the enclosed information (Example 10). If a punctuation mark immediately follows the second parentheses, no space is placed between the final parentheses and the punctuation mark (Example 10).

Example 10

The heart rate increased 12% more in the experimental group than in the control group (Figure 1). The change in blood pressure had no significant difference between the two groups (Figure 2).

1.7 Colon :

A colon signals that the information that follows is a further amplification of what was said before. The colon can also be used to introduce examples or members of the group being discussed (Example 11). Nevertheless, do not place a colon after a verb, because the verb also introduces and the colon would be redundant (Example 12). No space precedes a colon and one space follows it (Example 12).

Example 11

Three vital signs were recorded in the report: heart rate, respiration rate and blood pressure.

Example 12

Incorrect

The recorded vital signs were: heart rate, respiration rate and blood pressure.

1.8 Quotation Marks “ ”

Quotation marks are used to set apart a direct quote from an author or a speaker. They should be followed or preceded by a citation to the source of the quote. Quotation marks should not normally be used to set apart words or phrases within a sentence that are not direct quotes. Like parentheses, quotation marks have no space after the first or before the final quotation mark. One space is placed before the first and after the last quotation mark. In the United States, the convention is for ending periods or commas to fall within the final quotation mark (Example 13).

Example 13

Albert Einstein said: “I never teach my pupils. I only attempt to provide the conditions in which they can learn.”[1]

1.9 Suggestions on Correcting Punctuation and Spelling

Writing a paper with a word processing program helps to eliminate many common punctuation and spelling errors. If the automatic spelling/grammar check functions are activated, possible problems can be automatically highlighted and even corrected. Usually, by right-clicking the mouse

---

[1] From http://www.quotationspage.com/quotes/Albert_Einstein/

one time on the highlighted word, possible solutions will be provided. Then by left-clicking the appropriate solution one time, the text will be automatically corrected.

2. Capitalization

Capitalization can be a problem for writers whose native language has no capitalization, like Chinese. However, by following some simple rules, this problem can be easily solved. The rules below give some guidance on when to capitalize the first letter of a word.

2.1 The Beginning of Every Sentence

Every sentence begins with a capital letter. This may be one reason why numerals cannot be used at the beginning of a sentence (Example 14). If the sentence must begin with a number, the number must be written out (Example 15). An alternative would be to use an introductory phrase before the numeral (Example 16) or to rearrange the sentence structure (Example 17).

Example 14

Incorrect

10 samples were rejected because of insufficient records.

Example 15

Ten samples were rejected because of insufficient records.

Example 16

In total, 10 samples were rejected because of insufficient records.

Example 17

Because of insufficient records, 10 samples were rejected.

2.2 The First Letter of Every Main Word in a Title

Titles follow different rules other than the rest of the text. Titles do not need to be complete sentences, if the first word of a title is an article it can be omitted, and unless otherwise stipulated by the journal, the first letter of every word in the title should be capitalized, that is, the first letter of every word except for small words. This can be a little confusing, but usually all the words are capitalized except for articles, coordinating conjunctions and prepositions (Example 18). Of course, if the first word of a title is an article or a prepsition, the first letter must be capitalized.

Example 18

Effect of Smoking on Lung Cancer

2.3 Acronyms

Every letter of an acronym should be capitalized, whether it is an acronym that is pronounced like a word (AIDS) or an acronym in which the letters are pronounced one by one (NAACP). Unless the acronym is better known than its full form, write out the full form at first mention and place the acronym in parentheses. Writers must consider the limits of working memory when deciding how many acronyms to use in a passage. Use of acronyms should be limited to well-known forms and one or two unfamiliar forms that have multiple mentions.

2.4 Proper Nouns

The first letter of a proper noun is always capitalized. This includes the names of people, places, institutions and companies. If a person's title is followed by a name, then the title is also capitalized (Example 19); if not followed by a name, the title is not capitalized (Example 19). If a place name includes the article ***the***, the definite article is not capitalized (Example 19). The chemical names of medications are not capitalized (Example 20); however, manufacturers or brand names of medications are capitalized (Example 21).

Example 19

President Obama, the president of the United States, graduated from Columbia University.

Example 20

The patients were given 325 mg of acetaminophen daily.

Example 21

The patients were given 325 mg of Tylenol daily.

3. Key Points

- Nonstandard punctuation, capitalization or spelling interrupt the flow of the writing and should be found and corrected during editing.
- A word processing program is an indispensable tool for searching out and correcting problems with writing mechanics.

4. Revision Exercise

Direction: The following sentences are taken from an article written by Daniel Kahnemen. All punctuation and capitalization have been removed.

the operations of system 1 are fast automatic effortless associative and difficult to control or modify the operations of system 2 are slower serial effortful and deliberately controlled they are also relatively flexible and potentially rule-governed

Chapter Two Academic Style at the Phrase Level

Writing a phrase in an academic style involves using the words that express the intended meaning clearly and precisely, but also somewhat paradoxically, simply. When used properly, these three dimensions of communication check and balance each other, hopefully leading to the best choice of words.

1. Clarity

1.1 Articles (a/an, the, no article)

Clarity is often dependent on context, and the context of a noun phrase is set by the article or lack of article that precedes the noun. Improper usage of articles inevitably confuses and frustrates communication no matter how well the noun itself expresses the intended concept. The rules behind this seemingly simple choice are both numerous and complex (Yule, 2000), but there are some guidelines that can be followed to avoid many mistakes.

The key is to categorize the noun as countable or uncountable within the context that it is being used. If countable then it must be determined whether the noun is a singular or plural form and whether the noun describes a category or a particular member of a category.

Example 1

We randomly assigned patients to two different groups: medication group and placebo group.

In Example 1, **four** nouns must be analyzed: *patients, groups, group* and *group*. The first, ***patients***, is obviously both countable and plural because of the plural suffix **–s**. Therefore, now it must be determined whether the noun describes a category or a particular member of a category.

This depends on whether the concept of ***patients*** has already been identified in the previous sentence. If yes, then the noun refers to particular patients and the noun should be definite. To accomplish this with a plural countable noun, the article ***the*** should be used. If however, this is the first mention of the noun, then the sentence is expressing the type of subjects that were assigned (patients). If this is the case, the noun should be indefinite because its function is to categorize (define the type or category). With a plural countable noun, this is accomplished with ***no article*** and the noun phrase would be correct as written in the example.

The second noun, ***groups***, is also countable and plural as can be seen by the **–s** ending. By the context we can assume that this is the first mention of these two groups, so the noun's function is to categorize (indefinite), not to refer (definite). As explained in the previous paragraph, plural nouns with ***no article*** are indefinite.

The next noun in Example 1, ***group***, does not have a plural suffix, so its countability must be determined by the context. Since this particular group is one of the previously mentioned ***two groups***, it is safe to assume that this noun is also countable, but in this case singular. Again we must ask whether the noun introduces a category (type of group), or refers to a particular group. Since this noun is one of the previously mentioned ***two groups***, this phrase introduces a new subcategory and does not refer to a previously mentioned ***group***. With a singular, countable noun this is expressed with the indefinite article ***a (n)***. The next instance of the noun ***group*** can be analyzed in the same way and thus requires an indefinite article. In these last two cases, Example 1 is in error and the sentence should be revised as Example 2.

Example 2

We randomly assigned patients to two different groups: a medication group and a placebo group.

The next time that either the medication group or the placebo group are mentioned they will refer to the particular group and will require the definite article ***the***. The implication of this is that singular, countable nouns must be preceded by either ***a (n)*** or ***the*** and cannot function with ***no article*** (Example 3).

Example 3

Incorrect (Singular countable noun with no determiner)

Computer is a useful tool.

Correct (Definite article added)

The computer is a useful tool.

Correct (Plural-noun form with no determiner)

Computers are useful tools.

The last type of nouns that must be considered are uncountable or mass nouns. Because they are uncountable they only have one form and cannot be distinguished from singular countable nouns merely by their form. Like countable nouns, uncountable nouns either express a category (indefinite) or refer to an individual member of a category (definite). However, since they are uncountable they cannot take the article ***a (n)***. When expressing a category these nouns use ***no article*** (Example 4), and when referring to a particular member of a category they use the definite article ***the*** (Example 5). It is very important to remember that some nouns can be either countable or uncountable depending on the context. A normally uncountable noun that is being conceptualized as countable will use the indefinite article ***a (n)*** but will not have the same meaning as its uncountable, ***no article*** counterpart (Example 6).

Example 4

Medication was injected.

Example 5

The medication was injected.

Example 6

A medication was injected.

1.2 Modal Verbs

Like articles in a noun phrase, modal verbs set the context in a verb phrase. They can add a sense of obligation or responsibility (Example 7), predict behavior (Example 8), express ability (Example 9), express permission (Example 10), express choice (Example 11) or make a recommendation (Example 12) (Yule, 2000).

When used to express obligation, the appropriate use is determined by the type of relationship between the speaker and the listener. For instance, it would be inappropriate for a student to tell a teacher that the teacher ***should*** correct the student's homework; however, it may be entirely proper for the teacher to tell a student that the student ***should*** do so. In contrast, it would be proper for a student to ask a teacher if the teacher ***could*** correct the student's homework; however, it may be unwise for a teacher to ask a student if the student ***could*** correct the homework.

Example 7 (Obligation)

Doctors *should* treat patients kindly.

Doctors *must* treat patients kindly.

Example 8 (Prediction)

The doctor *might* arrive soon.

The doctor *may* arrive soon.

The doctor *should* arrive soon.

The doctor *must* arrive soon.

Example 9 (Ability)

The doctor *can* perform this technique.

Example 10 (Permission)

The doctor *can* use this drug now that it has been approved.

Example 11 (Choice)

The doctor *could* use this drug now that it has been approved.

Example 12 (Recommendation)

To avoid infection, doctors *should* wear a mask and gloves when treating patients.

When modal verbs are being used with verbs that express the action of inanimate objects, the modal verb can show ***possibility*** or ***probability***. It is useful to think of possibility as a binary choice, possible (Example 13) or not possible (Example 14), and to think of probability as a continuum of choices between the possible and the impossible (Example 15).

Example 13 (Possible)

The mechanism behind this correlation *could* be related to a third factor.

Example 14 (Impossible)

The mechanism behind this correlation *could not* be related to a third factor.

Example 15 (Probability)

The mechanism behind this correlation *must* be related to a third factor.

The mechanism behind this correlation *may* be related to a third factor.

The mechanism behind this correlation *might* be related to a third factor.

The mechanism behind this correlation *must* not be related to a third factor.

1.3 Adverb Placement

Although adverbs are moveable within a sentence, the meaning of the sentence does change when an adverb is moved. Look at the placement of '**significantly**' in the following three sentences.

- The heart rate increased *significantly* more in the experimental group than in the control group.
- The heart rate increased more *significantly* in the experimental group than in the control group.
- The heart rate *significantly* increased more in the experimental group than in the control group.

In Sentence 1, the difference between the increase in the experimental group and the increase in the control group is being compared and the difference was significant. In Sentence 2, the difference between the significance of the increase in the experimental group and the significance of the increase in the control group is being compared and the experimental group's significance was greater. In Sentence 3, the increase in both groups was also significant, but in this sentence the increase in the experimental group is being compared with the increase in the control group and the increase in the experimental group was greater. This differs from the first sentence in that the third sentence does not claim that the difference between the two increases was significant.

The key to understanding the change in meaning is to clarify what ***significantly*** and ***more*** are modifying. In the first sentence, ***significantly*** is modifying ***more***, and together they describe or modify the difference between the increase in the experimental group and the increase in the control group. The difference was significant. In the second sentence, the position of the two words has been switched and ***more*** is modifying ***significantly***. Together they are describing or modifying the increase in the experimental group, as compared to the control group. The significance was greater. In the third sentence ***significantly*** is modifying the verb ***increased***. The increase was significant and the increase was greater in the experimental group.

1.4 Noun Clusters

Noun clusters are extremely common in academic writing, and although they cannot be avoided, writers should be aware of them and try to limit their length (Zeiger, 1991). A noun cluster occurs when one or more nouns is moved to a position directly in front of another noun to function as an adjective (Example 16). It is important to understand that although it seems that the phrase has more than one noun, it does not. Only the final noun is actually functioning as a noun, and only the final noun can be treated as a noun. In Example 16 the noun ***heart*** is functioning as an adjective and not a noun. Notice how the verb agrees with the plural noun ***rates*** and not with ***heart***. In fact, because ***heart*** is functioning as an adjective, it cannot be made plural. Because of this, Example 17 is incorrect and must be revised in one of two ways (Example 18).

Example 16

The heart rates were continuously monitored throughout the study.

Example 17 (Incorrect)

Antibiotics abuse has caused an increase in antibiotics-resistant diseases.

Example 18

Antibiotic abuse has caused an increase in diseases that are resistant to antibiotics.

The abuse of antibiotics has caused an increase in diseases that are resistant to antibiotics.

2. Precision

Academic writing at the phrase level requires finding the most precise word available for expressing a concept or action. Notice how in Example 19 the meaning of the verb ***has*** seems to change depending on the subject of the verb. This ambiguity (more than one meaning) should be resolved by choosing a more precise verb (Example 20).

Example 19

The patient *has* surgery this afternoon.

The doctor *has* surgery this afternoon.

Example 20

The patient *undergoes* surgery this afternoon.

The doctor *performs* surgery this afternoon.

Nouns also exist on a continuum from more general to more specific. In addition, academic writing usually requires the noun that expresses the concept as specifically as possible. If a noun can be used to express different but similar concepts it is probably a category term and not very precise (Example 21). Thus, usually the more precise noun should be used (Example 22). The more general term can be used if two of the more precise concepts are being expressed in the same sentence (Example 23).

Example 21

The *level* of medication in the bottle was 4ml.

The *level* of medication in the bottle was 4ml/liter of saline.

The medication *level* of the bottle was 4ml.

Example 22

The *amount* of medication in the bottle was 4ml.

The *concentration* of medication in the bottle was 4ml/liter of saline.

The medication *content* of the bottle was 4ml.

Example 23

As the *amount* of medication increased, the *concentration* increased. Both *levels* exceeded the allowable standards.

3. Simplicity

When two different forms exist that clearly and precisely express the intended meaning, usually the simplest form is the best. **A good rule to follow:**

When a concept or relationship is complex, try to express it as simply as possible; when a concept or relationship is simple, do not artificially make it complex.

3.1 Fewer Words

In Example 24, the concept of ***male and female children*** is being expressed in such a way that requires one more word than the simpler and more common way of expressing the concept, ***boys and girls***. A word that is in common use is not necessarily unsuitable for academic writing; so if a concept can be expressed clearly with one word instead of two, then it probably should be so (Example 25).

Example 24

A total of *4 male* and *3 female children* were included in the study.

Example 25

A total of *4 boys* and *3 girls* were included in the study.

3.2 Contractions

Contractions (Example 26) are the written representation of an oral language form, and they should be avoided in academic writing. Always unpack the contraction and write out the complete form (Example 27).

Example 26

The degree of conformity to the enclosure *can't* be assumed.

Example 27

The degree of conformity to the enclosure *cannot* be assumed.

3.3 Abbreviations and Acronyms

The number of shortened terms used within a section should be controlled for the sake of the reader. Remembering one or two abbreviations or acronyms within a subsection or section is acceptable; however, every added shortened form makes reading exponentially more difficult for the reader. The exceptions are abbreviations and acronyms that are better known than the full form, for example DNA and SARS; however, it cannot be assumed that an abbreviation that is well known among specialists is universally well known.

4. Key Points

- Academic writing at the phrase level should be clear, precise and simple.
- Clarity can be achieved in noun phrases by careful choice of articles.
- Clarity can be achieved in verb phrases by careful choice of modal verbs.
- Ambiguity can be avoided by choosing the most precise phrase possible.
- Writers should not choose words that are unduly complex; choose the simplest form possible as long as the form is precise and clear.

5. Revision Exercise

Direction: Do the following exercises according to the specific requirement.

1) Do you think the following letter is appropriate for a doctor to give a patient's family member? If not, revise it.

The patient has presented with ascites and probable esophageal varices resulting from chronic hepatic failure. Diagnosis of the varices involves esophagogastroduodenoscopy; however, this could further exacerbate the condition by causing further hemorrhaging. The prognosis for this condition at this stage is not favorable. The patient should have begun treatment several years ago.

2) Which of the following sentences do you think is not in agreement with academic style? Why?

① Children with no father as a role model will become criminals.

② Children with no father as a role model may become criminals.

③ Children with no father as a role model could become criminals.

3) Rewrite the following noun clusters to express their meanings more clearly.

① filament length variability

② a hospital employee relations improvement program

4) Rewrite the following sentences to express their meanings more clearly and precisely.

① There were 41 hospitalizations, with similar numbers in the three day and five day treatments (18 and 23, respectively).

② Certain surgical procedures are known to be capable of inducing malignant tumors, although the ways in which this can happen have been classified as rare and very rare.

③ The effectiveness of mammographic screening for breast cancer depends on its ability to detect and to exclude the presence of breast cancer, measured as the sensitivity and specificity of mammography, respectively.

Chapter Three Academic Style at the Sentence Level

Academic style at the sentence level may be best understood through an analysis of the different elements within a sentence in terms of **function** and **grammar**. Once this has been accomplished, clear and concise sentences can be written by following a few simple rules.

1. Sentence Elements

1.1 The Subject

Rule 1: Make the topic of the sentence the subject of the sentence.

The topic of a sentence is what the sentence is about and can be expressed with a noun phrase. This noun phrase should usually be in the subject position. To convey information, a sentence must have both a topic and a message; so with the topic in the subject position, the remainder of the sentence or the clause will be used to provide further information about the topic, the message.

If the subject is used for a concept other than the topic, then the topic will be relegated to a minor role in the sentence, which is usually a mistake. In Example 1, the subject of the sentence is ***the patient***; however, it is unlikely that the topic of the sentence is ***the patient***. It is much more likely to be one of the either two important concepts, ***chemotherapy*** (Example 2), or ***cancer*** (Example 3). Notice how in the latter two examples, the cause and effect relationship between the chemotherapy and the remission is emphasized, rather than the relationship between the patient and the cancer that is emphasized in the first sentence.

Example 1

The patient experienced remission of cancer following 3 weeks of chemotherapy.

Example 2

Three weeks of chemotherapy resulted in a remission of cancer in the patient.

Example 3

The cancer went into remission following 3 weeks of chemotherapy by the patient.

1.2 The Action

Rule 2: Avoid Nominalizations.

A nominalization is a noun phrase that describes an action. A noun phrase that describes an action is appropriate if the action it describes is not being performed by the subject of the sentence. For instance, in Example 4, the noun ***exercise*** is the topic of the sentence, and although it describes an action, it should be the subject of the sentence. However, in Example 5, the subject of the sentence, ***my friend***, is performing the action, so the action should be described by a verb not a nominalization (Example 6) (Zeiger, 1991).

Example 4

Exercise can help to prolong life.

Example 5

My friend does exercise every day.

Example 6

My friend exercises every day.

Rule 3: Avoid Unnecessary Words.

A concise sentence is a sentence in which every element has a necessary function. Finding and eliminating any unnecessary elements and functions is an important part of the revision process. By paying attention to several danger areas, this can eventually become a natural part of the writing process.

2. Topic Comment Structures

Although topics have a prominent position in the sentences of some languages, topic comment structures are relatively rare and should be avoided in English (Finegan E, 1999; Gass, M, Selinker L, 2008; Gee, 1985). In Example 7, the topic of the sentence has been marked with the ***as for...*** construction. However, this makes it necessary to use the pronoun ***it*** in the subject position. Notice how the sentence becomes both shorter and more powerful by eliminating the introductory phrase (Example 8).

Example 7

As for medical education, it has experienced profound development over the past decade.

Example 8

Medical education has experienced profound development over the past decade.

3. Unnecessary Adverbials

Much of the necessary context is provided by the verb tense and aspect in English. Because of this, setting up context through adverbials that modify the sentence is often unnecessary and redundant. In fact, the extra markers can sometimes take the emphasis away from what is most important in a sentence. In Example 9, the use of ***It is well known*** shifts the emphasis from the message to the fact that the message is known. If this is not the intention of the sentence the clause should be omitted (Example 10). In Example 11, the message becomes further confused by the addition of a clause that is probably not even literally true, ***We all know that.*** Again, if the intention of the sentence is to establish the relationship between the two variables and not to establish that the relationship is common knowledge, Example 10 is by far the best choice.

Example 9

It is well known that obesity is a common cause of diabetes.

Example 10

Obesity is a common cause of diabetes.

Example 11

We all know that obesity is a common cause of diabetes.

Adverbials of time are also often unnecessary and may take away the impact of the actual message of the sentence. In Example 12, it is implied that the message applies to the present. Because of this, the addition of ***Nowadays*** is unnecessary. Notice how the message becomes more powerful when the distracting addition has been omitted (Example 13).

Example 12

Nowadays, technology has become an important tool for education.

Example 13

Technology has become an important tool for education.

The goal is to express the message as clearly and powerfully as possible. This is often accomplished best by eliminating any unnecessary elements that could divert attention away from the core message.

4. Key Points

- Academic style at the sentence level can be achieved by making the topic of the sentence the subject of the sentence, by expressing the action of the sentence through the verb, and by avoiding unnecessary words.
- The topic-comment structures found in Chinese sentences should be avoided in English.
- Adverbial phrases and clauses should not be used unless they are providing essential, non-repetitive information to the sentence.

5. Revision Exercise

Direction: Do the following exercises according to the specific requirement.

1) The following sentence requires revision before being used in an academic text.

As for smoking, it has long been known that it has a function of causing respiratory disease.

2) Analyze the following four sentences. Which one is the best example in the academic style? Illustrate your choice.

① We wish to suggest a structure for the salt of DNA that has novel features that are of considerable biological interest.

② We wish to suggest a structure for the salt of deoxyribose nucleic acid (DNA). It has novel features which are of considerable biological interest.

③ We wish to suggest a structure for the salt of deoxyribose nucleic acid (DNA). This configuration has novel features which are of considerable biological interest.

④ We wish to suggest a structure for the salt of deoxyribose nucleic acid (DNA). This structure has novel features which are of considerable biological interest.

Chapter Four Academic Style at the Paragraph Level

Academic writing at the paragraph level is similar to academic writing at the sentence level in that the structure should be determined by the function of some essential elements. A well-written paragraph should, like a sentence, have **a clear topic** and **message**.

1. The Topic Sentence

The foundation for the organization of a paragraph is established through the first sentence, the topic sentence (Strunk, 2006). The name ***topic sentence***, however, is somewhat misleading. The function of this sentence is not to provide the topic of the paragraph, but to provide both the topic and the message of the paragraph.

Because the topic sentence provides the topic and message for the paragraph, it sets the boundaries for what can be discussed in the paragraph. This can be illustrated with **three simple and useful rules.**

Rule 1: The subject of the topic sentence should be the topic of the paragraph.

Rule 2: The message of the topic sentence should match the message of the paragraph's content.

Rule 3: Every sentence in the paragraph should be a further explanation of the message of the topic sentence.

If a student were assigned to write a paragraph about ***how to cook tomato and eggs***, any of the following three topic sentences could be imagined. However, only one of the three sentences obeys the three rules for a well written topic sentence.

1. The topic of this paragraph is *How to cook tomato and eggs*.
2. Tomato and eggs is a delicious and popular Chinese dish.
3. Cooking tomato and eggs requires five ingredients and five steps.

The first sentence violates Rule 1, because the subject of the sentence is the word ***topic*** and it does not express what the paragraph is about. The paragraph is not about ***topics***. The second sentence, ***tomato and eggs***, almost obeys Rule 2 in that the subject of the sentence expresses something about the topic of the paragraph (the name of the dish); however, the sentence breaks Rule 2 because the message of the sentence is not the message of the paragraph. The paragraph will be about how the dish is cooked, not about the taste and popularity of the dish.

The third sentence is the only possible choice because the subject of the sentence matches the topic of the paragraph and the message of the sentence matches what the content of the paragraph should include. Thus if all of the sentences that follow this topic sentence are further details about the five ingredients and five steps, the topic sentence and paragraph will match. Moreover, if these details are logically ordered, the paragraph will be well written.

2. The Order of Details

The order of the details that follow the topic sentence should be logical, efficient and effective. The order will be logical if it follows a predetermined plan or rule such as order of importance, order of physical location or chronological order (time sequence order). If no ordering scheme seems to apply, then the details should be ordered in such a way that their mention is consistent with the topic sentence (announced order).

The order of the details will be efficient if they allow for a minimum of repetition. For instance, in Example 1 the author has chosen chronological order and the choice has resulted in repetition. Ordering the details from the most to the least important results in a much more efficient expression of the procedure (Example 2), because of the elimination of repetition.

Example 1

The patient was given a total dose of 100 milligrams aspirin. First, the patient's blood pressure and body temperature were measured and recorded, followed by a control period of thirty minutes. And then aspirin (50 mg) was given to the patient. One hour later the patient's blood pressure and body temperature were measured again. Thirty minutes later the final dose of aspirin (50 mg) was given.

Example 2

The patient was given a total of 100 milligrams of aspirin in two consecutive doses. The first dose (50 mg) was given one hour before the second dose (50 mg). Before each dose, the patient's blood pressure and temperature were recorded followed by a thirty minute control period.

A paragraph is effective if the most important details stand out from the rest. This can be done by placing the important details in prominent positions in the sentence and paragraph. In Example 3, a strict chronological order is used and thus ***no detail feels*** more important than the others.

Example 3

First, the patient's blood pressure was measured and then his body temperature was taken. Thirty minutes later, the patient was given 50 mg aspirin. Finally, the patient's blood pressure and body temperature were measured once more and thirty minutes later, the patient was given a second 50 mg dose of aspirin.

By using the topic sentence to express the most important topic and message, this message will be established as the focus of the paragraph. In addition, if the details that follow are sequenced from the most to the least important, then that variable will continue to stand out from among the others. In Example 4, the subject of the topic sentence is the blood pressure measurement and it immediately becomes the focus of the paragraph. The following two sentences place the administration of aspirin in a subordinate position to the blood pressure measurement (Compare with Example 2). Finally, the measurement of body temperature is mentioned at the end of the paragraph in the weakest position.

Example 4

The patient's blood pressure was taken and recorded twice. Thirty minutes after the first measurement the patient was given 50 mg aspirin, directly followed by the second measurement. Thirty minutes after the second measurement the patient was again given 50 mg aspirin. At the time of both blood pressure measurements, the patient's body temperature was measured and recorded.

By reading and comparing the Examples 1 through 4, it becomes clear how important it is to establish the main topic and message within a paragraph.

3. The Consistency

The concept of consistency forces the writer to consider how writing choices may affect the reader. The goal is not to surprise the reader with any sudden shifts in time, space or logic, and this is accomplished through the manipulation of verb tense and sentence topics. In Example 5 the sudden shift from past to present tense between the first and second sentences illustrates an inconsistent and confusing shift in time.

Example 5

The purpose of this study was to test the hypothesis that stress is associated with absenteeism among urban commuters. To test this hypothesis 1,000 commuters are questioned about stress levels and work habits.

Avoiding confusing shifts in time does not mean that every verb in a paragraph must have the same tense, but it does mean that the verb tense should be chosen in such a way that the reader does not experience a sudden shift in time. For instance, in the first sentence of Example 5 it is correct that the description of the hypothesis remains in the present tense (***is associated***) even though the main verb of the sentence is in the past tense (***was***). For further explanation of tense in the hypothesis, see Chapter Eight.

Consistency is established through verb tense and is established through the manipulation of sentence topics. An analysis of sentence topics in Example 6 reveals an inconsistent flow of topics. The topic of the first sentence, what the sentence is about, is ***questionnaires***. The topic of the second sentence is ***commuters***, and the topic of the third sentence is ***answers***. Taking a step back reveals how these three concepts relate to the study. The first, ***questionnaires***, represents the methodology, the second, ***commuters***, represents the population, and the third, ***answers***, represents the data gathered. This shift in topics results in an uncomfortable shift for the reader and interrupts the smooth flow of ideas. The easiest way to resolve this problem would be to determine which element is the most important, and to keep this variable in the forefront as the sentence topics progress through the paragraph. (Example 6).

Example 6

To test the hypothesis that stress is associated with absenteeism in urban commuters, questionnaires were used to measure the stress levels and work habits of 1,000 commuters. The commuters who had agreed to take part in the study were read questions during the morning commute. The answers were then recorded and later analyzed and compared to determine the existence of correlations between indexes of stress levels and absenteeism.

In the revised version (Example 7), the topics of the first sentence are ***stress levels and work habits***. It could be argued that these two concepts are the most important variables because they represent the dependent and independent variables within the hypothesis, ***stress and absenteeism***. The second sentence has two choices for topics: the sentence can be about the questions, or about the commuters. By choosing ***questions*** as the topic of the second sentence, two things are accomplished. A smooth transition takes place from the last word of the first sentence, ***questionnaires***, to the subject and topic of the second sentence, ***the questions*** and a more consistent flow of topics is maintained by not choosing the population as the topic of the sentence. The third sentence has at least three choices for topics: indexes of stress levels and absenteeism, answers and existence of correlations. To preserve the original choice of topics from the first sentence, ***Indexes of stress levels and absenteeism*** was chosen as the topic of the final sentence. However, it could probably be argued that to preserve the flow of ideas from the topic of the previous sentence (The questions), ***answers***, could possibly be the best choice as topic and subject of the final sentence (Example 7 in parentheses).

Example 7

To test the hypothesis that stress is associated with absenteeism in urban commuters, the stress levels and work habits of 1,000 commuters were measured through questionnaires. The questions were read to commuters who had agreed to take part in the study during their morning commute. Indexes of stress levels and absenteeism were then calculated from the answers, analyzed and compared to determine the existence of correlations.

(The answers were then recorded and later analyzed and compared to determine the existence of correlations between indexes of stress levels and absenteeism.)

A well-written paragraph does not automatically come naturally, even for native speakers.

Analysis and conscious choices must be made. By taking some time to establish the topic and message in a well-written topic sentence, and then by ordering the details in the most logical, efficient and effective way a smooth and consistent flow of ideas can be realized.

4. The Point of View

For the most part, the point of view is not a complicated issue in academic writing. The point of view should be that of 3rd person. This means that the writer and the reader (1st and 2nd person) should not become part of the text through first- or second-person pronouns like ***I*** or ***you***. However, this also means that the reader should not be addressed through direct questions (Example 8). Any questions should be reworded to exclude the reader (Example 9).

Example 8

What could be the cause of this relationship?

Example 9

The cause of this relationship is unknown.

The exception to the exclusive use of the third person in a research paper is within sections in which methodology is being discussed. It is acceptable to use the first-person plural pronoun (we) as the subject of sentences describing methods (Zeiger, 1991). However, once this decision has been made the writer should be careful to maintain a consistent flow of topics. In sentences one and two of Example 10 the topics of the sentences are the methodology (***We measured, We read***). However, the topic of the third sentence is the data gathered (***the answers***). By changing the subject of this sentence to match the previous sentences a consistent point of view can be maintained (Example 11).

Example 10

To test the hypothesis that stress is associated with absenteeism in urban commuters, we measured the stress levels and work habits of 1,000 commuters through questionnaires. We read the questions to commuters who had agreed to take part in the study during the morning commute. The answers were then recorded and later analyzed and compared to determine the existence of correlations between indexes of stress levels and absenteeism.

Example 11

To test the hypothesis that stress is associated with absenteeism in urban commuters, we measured the stress levels and work habits of 1,000 commuters through questionnaires. We read the questions to commuters who had agreed to take part in the study during the morning commute. We then recorded and later analyzed and compared the answers to determine the existence of correlations between indexes of stress levels and absenteeism.

A comparison of Example 7 and Example 11 reveals a choice between many sentences with passive voice verbs, and many sentences with ***We*** as a subject. This can be looked at as a decision that must be made between two not very good choices. The key is to try to remain consistent within the paragraph once the choice has been made and to either emphasize the subjects, materials or variables through the use of passive voice verbs (Example 7) or to emphasize the methods used through the choice of ***We*** as subject (Example 11).

5. Key Points

- Academic writing at the paragraph level can be achieved by the careful use of topic sentences.
- The subject of the topic sentence should be the topic of the paragraph.
- The message of the topic sentence should match the message of the paragraph.
- Every sentence in the paragraph should be directly related to the message of the topic sentence.
- The order of the details following the topic sentence should be logical and should emphasize the most important points.
- Consistency can be achieved through verb tense, the careful choice of sentence topics and a consistent point of view.

6. Revision Exercise

Direction: Do the following exercises according to the specific requirement.

1) The following paragraph needs revision before it could be used in an academic text.

Four hundred healthy, willing and age-matched participants were randomly and evenly divided into a facemask or a non-facemask group. The facemask group wore a cotton facemask throughout their public commute time and the non-facemask group wore no covering over their faces. At the end of 60 days, we compared the incidence of viral infections between the two groups.

2) Please revise the following paragraph to make its order of details more logical, efficient, and effective.

【A】A full moon occurs about 12 times a year and has always been drawing people's attention from the past to the present, causing possible traffic problems.【B】A full moon might lead to changes in surrounding traffic behaviors, such as drawing the attention from other motorists or pedestrians from noticing an oncoming motorcycle.【C】The primary cause of motorcycle crashes is glancing at a full moon takes the motorcyclist's gaze off the road, which could result in a loss of control.【D】We hypothesized that because people's attention is naturally drawn to a full moon, it might contribute to fatal motorcycle crashes.

3) Please identify the problem(s) in the following paragraph and then revise it.

We did a systematic search for relevant articles published between 1960 and restricted to the English language. We considered studies if they evaluate association between macronutrient intake and total mortality or cardiovascular disease. The studies cited in this report were not an exhaustive list of existing research.

Chapter Five Correspondence

Writing to an individual through a letter or email is constrained by different principles than writing to a broad audience for a publication. Therefore, it should not be surprising that writing correspondence has its own rules and conventions. Although an academic style can be appropriate for correspondence between academics, the relationship between the writer and reader must be considered and preserved through the language choices. In fact, the **relationship** is the most important factor when writing correspondence; even more important than the reason the letter is being written in the first place. If the relationship cannot be established and preserved, it is very unlikely that the correspondence will achieve the hoped-for results.

1. Relationship Types

Two different models can be used to help make conscious decisions about the appropriate language within correspondence: a model for relationship types and a model for perceived identities. One model for relationship types written about and used by many anthropologists categorizes individual relationships by one of four guiding principles: ***authority ranking; market pricing; equality or communal sharing*** (Fiske, 1992).

Examples for each category are easy to imagine: a boss can tell an employee what to do (***authority ranking***); a taxi driver expects fair payment for giving a ride to a commuter (***market pricing***); a teacher expects a favor in return for taking over a colleague's class for the day (***equality***); and parents get as much joy as the child when they give a daughter or son a gift (***communal sharing***).

It is easy to see how the same behavior may have different meanings in the context of these four different relationship types. Behavior such as gift-giving may be interpreted by a doctor as bribery, may be interpreted by a taxi driver as a gratuity for good service, may be interpreted by a colleague as a prelude for a request for a return favor, and may be interpreted by a child as an expression of love. The same behavior elicits four different meanings, and for the relationship to be preserved the interpreted meaning must match the intended meaning; e.g., if a gift to a doctor was meant by a patient as an expression of appreciation, but was interpreted by the doctor as a bribe, problems will surely arise between the doctor and patient.

2. Identity

When problems do arise, it is often because of a shock to the perceived identity of the recipient. Identity is a complex concept that encapsulates how a person perceives him/herself. A useful model for analyzing identity incorporates four categories that correspond to four strands within each person's perceived sense of self: natural, institutional, affinity, and earned identities (Gee, 2000-2001). **Natural identity** is the strand of self-perception related to the attributes given by nature: birthplace, gender, hair color, etc. **Institutional identity** is related to the attributes given through a higher authority: driver's license, PhD degree, residence certificate, etc. **Affinity identity** is related to the attributes chosen out of interest: hobbies, pastimes, entertainment choices. **Earned identity** is related to the attributes obtained through study or practice: doctor, teacher, piano player.

When people are confronted with words and behavior that contradict their perceived self identity they will respond to this contradiction. For example, one famous actor in the US was able to devise a costume that allowed him to shop and eat in public places unrecognized. He soon abandoned the practice because it was too difficult for him to be treated like a normal person by shop clerks and waiters. Their behavior contradicted his sense of self as a celebrity, and he found it to be an uncomfortable experience.

Similarly, a doctor who feels that he is being bribed will experience a shock to his identity if he feels that an integral part of his earned identity is built on a moral and ethical foundation. The patient's image of the doctor's professional self does not fit his own and a communication breakdown is inevitable unless this issue can be resolved. Most misunderstandings are not as dramatic as the above examples; however, academic and professional correspondence often involve some relatively important issues, and for the correspondence to have its intended effect, the relational and identity dimensions need to be considered.

3. Using the Appropriate Language

A student writing to a past professor to request a letter of reference must first place the language of the letter within the boundaries of the student's relationship with the professor and the professor's sense of self within this relationship. In addition, any request or offer made must be appropriate within these boundaries.

The relationship will probably be best described as an ***authority ranking*** relationship, with the professor holding authority or power over the student. The authority will be based on power derived from the ***institution*** in which the professor taught and the student learned, and from the respect ***earned*** by the professor for reaching that level within the institution. Thus, both ***institutional*** and ***earned*** identity strands will be engaged as the professor reads the correspondence. Engaging these identity strands within this type of relationship requires a humble and thankful attitude on the part of the writer.

The humble and thankful attitude runs throughout Example 1 and because of this the goal for the correspondence is much more likely to be achieved. The first sentence introduces the writer in the context of their past relationship as teacher-student. However, although the main function of the sentence is the introduction it does so with a humble and grateful attitude with the phrase ***privileged to be***. If this phrase is removed (Example 2), the necessary attitude is lost and the sentence becomes cold and objective. Before explaining the reason for the letter, the writer expresses appreciation and then gradually leads to the request. The request is couched in the most polite and gracious manner possible, ***I was hoping that you could find the time***. This expresses that the writer understands that the request will inconvenience the reader, and that the reader's time is valuable. It also clearly communicates that the reader is in control of the choice to grant the request or not. In no way is the writer assuming that the reader is obligated. The information about the enclosed form also makes no presumption on the part of the writer because of the introductory phrase, ***if so***. In Example 2, this is not so. By removing the humble and thankful attitude, the letter becomes more of a demand than a request, and it is very possible that the letter will not achieve its intended purpose.

Example 1

Dear Professor Smith:

My name is John Paul and I was privileged to be a student in your Philosophy 405 class in the fall of 2018.

First, I want to express my appreciation for your teaching and let you know how much that course has influenced and helped me. This brings me to the reason for this letter. I have been given the opportunity to continue my studies in philosophy in the pursuit of a Masters of Arts degree. I was hoping that you could find the time to provide a letter of reference as part of the admission procedure. If so, I have enclosed the form and necessary information for submitting the letter.

Again, I want to extend my thanks for all you have done to help me to advance in my studies.

Sincerely,

John Paul

Example 2

Dear Professor Smith:

My name is John Paul and I was a student of yours in your Philosophy 405 class in the fall of 2018. I have been given the opportunity to continue my studies in philosophy in the pursuit of a Masters of Arts degree. Could you provide a letter of reference as part of the admission procedure? I have enclosed the form and necessary information for submitting the letter.

Sincerely,

John Paul

The same request within a different relationship type will be written quite differently. A request for a letter of reference from a colleague will be constrained by a relationship based on ***equality*** rather than ***authority ranking***. This equality will be based on the institutionally earned power as in the previous example; however, in this case no imbalance of power exists. This letter should reflect this balance.

The first three sentences in Example 3 establish personal connections rather than professional connections. Whereas, this would be entirely inappropriate in an unbalanced relationship such as the previous example, it is appropriate and necessary for making a request within an equal relationship. The request is expressed as ***a favor***, which expresses well the act of doing something for a friend or colleague. A favor implies that the favor will be returned someday, which is reflected in the offer to buy dinner at the end of the paragraph. By comparing Example 2 and Example 3 it becomes obvious that the request itself is a minor part of such a letter; the majority of the phrases and sentences are used to manage the relationship.

Example 3

Dear Sam:

I am sorry that we haven't had a chance to get together lately. I imagine that you have been as busy, or busier than I have been. I hope that all is well with your family.

The reason I am writing is that I want to ask a favor. I am applying for a grant that requires several reference letters from colleagues. Could you help me out and send one according to the form that I have attached? If you could, I would really appreciate it. I hope that we can finally get together for dinner soon and it will be on me. Let me know when you will be in the area.

Yours truly,

Richard

4. Cover Letters

4.1 The Function

The function of a cover letter is somewhat like that of the abstract, in that a cover letter introduces the main findings of a manuscript; however, it has some unique functions as well: the cover letter should communicate why the manuscript is suited to the specific journal. In addition, the cover letter should introduce the authors, the corresponding author and the contact information. Finally, the journal itself may have special requirements for the cover letter; possibly even concerning specific wording within the cover letter. These requirements may include statements that the authors approved the manuscript and that the manuscript has not been submitted to any other journals.

4.2 The Overall Structure

Whether in printed or electronic format the cover letter should follow the format of a standard business letter. All information should be justified on the left of the page, beginning with the date, and then followed by the editor's name, journal name and address, salutation, body, closing and signature block.

4.3 The Salutation

The salutation should be directed to the editor of the journal if the editor's name is not known

(Example 4). If the editor's name is known, see the editor's title and family name (Example 5).

Example 4

Dear Editor:

Example 5

Dear Dr. Smith:

4.4 The Body

The body of the cover letter should normally include four paragraphs. The first paragraph should begin with a sentence that introduces the corresponding author's name, and the title of the abstract. The second paragraph should outline the findings and their importance. Try to connect these findings to the goals of the journal of submission. The third paragraph should include any specific statements required by the journal, and the final paragraph should close with an expression of gratitude for considering the manuscript. The entire cover letter should not be more than one page.

4.5 The Closing

The cover letter should end with a simple closing and a signature block, followed by the corresponding author's name and contact information (Example 6). Remember that different journals have different requirements. Following these requirements is the most important element of a successful cover letter. At the same time, keep in mind the need to emphasize the importance and the relevance of the findings to the journal of submission. The final step is to reread the cover letter and remove any unnecessary or redundant language.

Example 6

Sincerely,

John Smith, Ph.D.

Institution

Street Address

City, Province Postal Code

Email Address

Phone Number

5. Replies to Reviewers

When replying to reviewers it is important to avoid becoming defensive. Consider the criticism as valuable insight into how the paper would be received after publication, and a valuable opportunity to improve the paper before this takes place. With this attitude, be thankful to the reviewers for their helpful (as well as not so helpful) insights and respond to the points one by one by making the necessary changes, not by defending the original. If the reviewer misunderstood the original intention, then that must mean that it was not stated clearly enough and that changes should be made.

6. Samples

6.1 Cover Letters

A. Letter One

Dear Editor:

We would like to submit our manuscript titled "**Imaging Superoxide Flash and Metabolism-coupled Mitochondrial Permeability Transition in Living Animals**" for consideration as an Article to ***Science***.

Recently we discovered that transient mitochondrial permeability transition (tMPT) triggers "superoxide flashes", the quantal events of mitochondrial reactive oxygen species (ROS) production in normal cells (Green et al. ***Cell***, 2006, 112: 241.). This breakthrough challenges the conventional view of MPT by suggesting the physiological relevance of tMPT in ROS signaling and normal cell function. To provide unequivocal evidence supporting this hypothesis, it is absolutely necessary to seek in vivo approaches to monitor superoxide flash in living animals, a real physiological condition compared to cultured cells or tissues. Here, we report the first in vivo molecular imaging technique for evaluating mitochondrial ROS signals and tMPT activities. Further, taking advantage of this novel technique, we uncovered the metabolism-tMPT-superoxide flash coupling in live animals bearing the newly developed superoxide indicator. Our major findings are:

1. Imaging tMPT/superoxide flashes in living animals at the single mitochondrion resolution. We generated superoxide indicator-expressing transgenic mouse lines and developed novel *in vivo* imaging technique that enabled real-time investigation of tMPT/superoxide flash in multiple tissues of anesthetized mice.

2. tMPT/superoxide flash production is a fundamental and universal property of mitochondria function *in vivo*. We have, for the first time, demonstrated robust tMPT/superoxide flash activity in skeletal muscle and sciatic nerve trunk in live animals, a truly physiological context. That tMPT is a house-keeping event contrasts to the prevalent view that sustained MPT (sMPT) induces apoptosis.

3. Synchronized tMPT/superoxide flashes reveal three-dimensional functional mitochondrial network *in vivo*. By fast 4D (*xyz-t*) imaging, we portrayed synchronous superoxide flashes in three-dimensions, and provided perhaps the first demonstration of functional mitochondrial network in intact cells. Evidence was provided supporting tMPT as a common triggering mechanism, and physical connectivity may account for functional integration in a local mitochondrial network.

4. Coupling of mitochondrial metabolism to tMPT/superoxide flash activity in living animals. Superoxide flash activity surged in response to systemic administration of glucose or insulin in mice, in an apparently frequency-modulated (FM) mode. Punctiform and network mitochondria respond similarly to metabolic stimulation. These findings reveal a fundamental link between mitochondrial metabolism and tMPT activity and quantal superoxide signaling.

5. We propose that FM-control of intermittent tMPT activity can provide an efficient means for metabolic regulation and coordination between metabolism and local ROS signaling. In our opinion, this represents a paradigm-shifting advance in delineating physiologically the roles of tMPT and mitochondrial ROS signaling. As well, it bears far-reaching implications in understanding the pathogenesis and devising the treatment of a wide variety of metabolic disorders and oxidative stress-related diseases.

6. Increased tMPT/superoxide flash activity underlies oxidative stress during in vivo ischemia / reperfusion treatment. During the skeletal muscle ischemia / reperfusion treatment in vivo, we demonstrated the altered tMPT/superoxide flash activities in accordance to muscle oxygen supply. Significant and prolonged increase in superoxide flash frequency during reperfusion manifested the critical role of mitochondrial derived ROS in oxidative damage of the muscle.

As mitochondrial and ROS are regaining the central stage of biomedicine, we are very excited about the prospect that our novel technology will be widely applicable to understanding mitochondrial biology and physiology, delineating roles of mitochondrial ROS in the pathogenesis of a large panel of diseases (metabolic disorders, cardiovascular and neurodegenerative disease, cancer), and assessing medicinal, cell and gene therapies. We wish you will share the enthusiasm in reviewing and publishing these findings.

Sincerely,

Peter Green, Ph.D.

University Professor, Michigan University

PS: please see the list of four potential expert referees on a separate sheet.

B. Letter Two

Dear Dr. Prendergast,

Please find the enclosed a manuscript titled "**Hypoxia-inducible factor-2 activation promotes colorectal cancer progression through regulation of tumor iron homeostasis**", that we wish to be considered for publication in *Cancer Research*.

Hypoxia is a hallmark of solid tumors. Hypoxic signal transduction is mediated by two transcription factors HIF-1 and HIF-2. In the present manuscript, we demonstrate through mouse models that HIF-2 is a critical transcription factor that is essential for the initiation and progression of colorectal carcinogenesis.

We show that chronic activation of HIF-2 increases colon carcinogenesis through dysregulation of the local iron homeostasis. These data provide a mechanistic basis for the widely reported link between iron accumulation and colon cancer incidence. The present study identifies a novel role for HIF-2 in initiating a coordinated process that is critical in progression of colon cancer. Therefore, the data implicates HIF-2 as potential target for the prevention and treatment of colon cancer.

We look forward to hearing from you on the outcome of our manuscript review.

Best wishes,

Alexander Garruss Ph.D.

6.2 Replies to Reviewers

C. Letter Three

RE: Submission of revised manuscript for publication in *Journal of Hepatology*

Dear Professors Moreau and Samuel:

Please find attached copy of an amended version of our manuscript titled "Role of Myc in hepatocellular proliferation and hepatocarcinogenesis". My colleagues and I thank you and the reviewers for your time and efforts in reviewing our manuscript. The comments of the editors and reviewers are greatly appreciated. We have addressed each of the concerns that were raised by the reviewers, and revised the manuscript accordingly. For your convenience, following is a point-by-point response to the reviewers' comments.

Sincerely,

Frank Adam Wilson, Ph.D.

Dean, Laboratory of Metabolism

National Cancer Institute

Response to Reviewer 1

Major comments:

In their study, Qu et al. reported a liver-specific myc deletion mouse model. Using this model, they deciphered the role of myc in proliferation (using PPARalpha agonist) and liver carcinogenesis (using DEN carcinogen). It is an interesting study that highlighted the pleiotropic role of myc in the liver.

Response: We appreciate the positive comments from the reviewer.

Specific comments:

1. The authors stated that myc is "not required for PPARalpha dependent fatty acid beta oxidation" (page 9) and that myc deletion "did not alter the expression of genes involved in glucose metabolism, nor the genes responsible for glutamin metabolism" (page 15). However, microarray analysis of myc$^{-/-}$ *liver treated by PPARalpha agonist revealed that carbohydrate and lipid metabolism related genes are upregulated (table 1). It should be discusses by the authors.*

Response: We thought Myc was not necessary for glutamine metabolism due to no difference of major genes involved in glutamine metabolism upon PPARalpha agonist treatment as the figure below shows. However, in accordance with the reviewer's suggestion, we added discussion on page 15 that "Myc disruption may increase the beta-oxidation-independent carbohydrate and lipid metabolism via an indirect regulatory pathway. This will be further investigated".

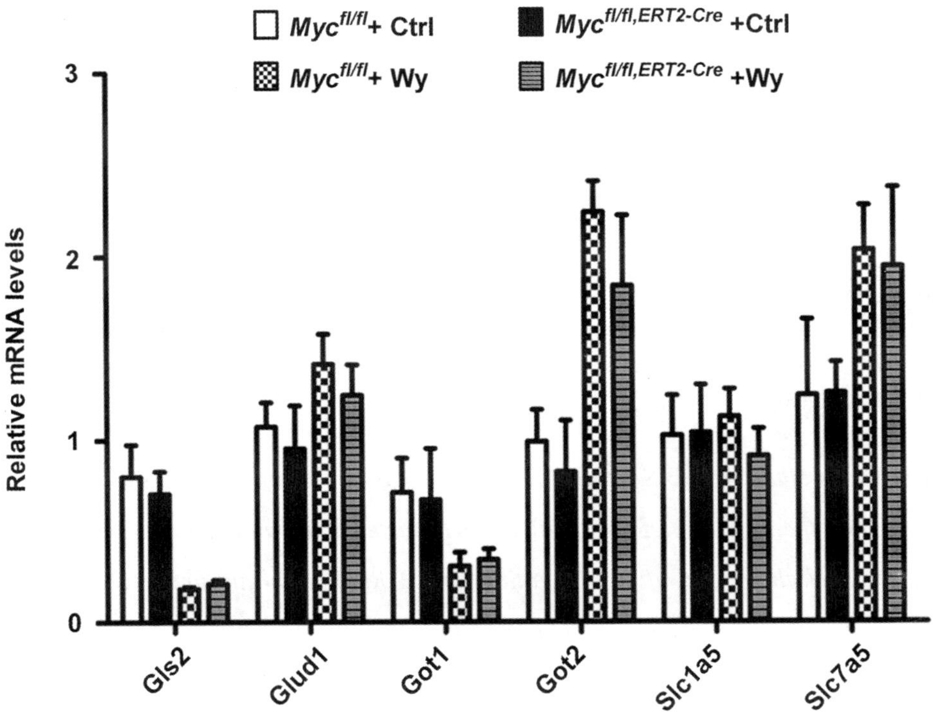

Figure legend: mRNA levels of genes involved in glutamine metabolism upon 2 days-Wy-14, 643 treatment. Values were means ± SD. $n = 6 - 8$ per group.

2. It should be interesting to assess KI67 or PCNA immunostaining in liver tumors induced by DEN in myc$^{-/-}$ compared to myc$^{fl/fl}$ mouse. As myc regulates non-tumor hepatocytes proliferations, we could hypothesize that tumor hepatocyte proliferation is reduced in myc$^{-/-}$ mouse treated by DEN.

Response: We performed the Ki67 IHC staining with the liver tumors in *Myc*$^{F/F}$ and *Myc*$^{F/F;\ ERT2\text{-}Cre}$ mouse and found that the hepatocyte proliferation was reduced in *Myc*$^{F/F;\ ERT2\text{-}Cre}$ mouse treated by DEN as expected. We included this result in Figure 4F.

3. The authors have to check if myc deletion is maintained in tumor hepatocytes in myc$^{-/-}$ mouse treated by DEN. Maybe tumor hepatocytes escape to myc deletion and could explain that a small proportion of tumors (33%) developed in myc deleted liver.

Response: We extracted the genomic DNA from adjacent non-tumor and tumor tissue from DEN-treated *Myc*$^{F/F;\ ERT2\text{-}Cre}$ mice. We found a slight non-recombinant *Myc*-floxed band in the tumor. Thus, we agree with the reviewer that DEN-induced tumor hepatocytes could escape *Myc* disruption by unknown mechanisms; this could explain the small proportion of tumors developed in $Myc^{F/F;\ ERT2\text{-}Cre}$ mice. An example of two tumors is shown below.

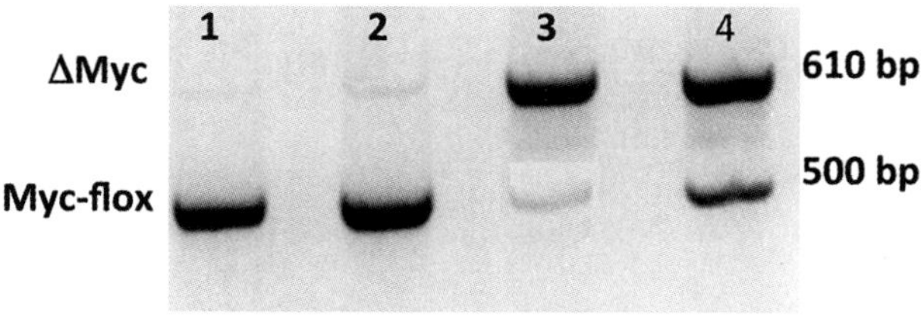

Figure legend: PCR analysis for *Myc*-allele recombination of genomic DNA from DEN-treated $Myc^{fl/fl}$ and $Myc^{fl/fl,\ ERT2\text{-}Cre}$ mice. Lane 1, non-tumor tissue from DEN-treated $Myc^{fl/fl}$ liver; lane 2, tumor tissue from DEN-treated $Myc^{fl/fl}$ liver; lane 3, non-tumor tissue from DEN-treated $Myc^{fl/fl,\ ERT2\text{-}Cre}$ liver; lane 4, tumor from DEN-treated $Myc^{fl/fl,\ ERT2\text{-}Cre}$ liver.

4. A previous study (Cairo S, et al. PNAS 2010) has shown that myc could regulate the miR-371-3 cluster and the miR-100/let-7a-2/miR-125b-1 cluster in hepatoblastoma and HCC. It will be interesting to check their level after stimulation by PPARalpha and in tumors induced by DEN in the hepatocyte specific $myc^{-/-}$ *mouse model proposed by the authors.*

Response: We previously did not consider the miR-290-295 cluster (homolog of human miR-371-3 in mouse) or miR-100/let-7a-2/miR-125b-1 cluster due to an unpublished microRNA array on Wy-14, 643-treated and untreated livers, in which no significant changes were detected with the above miRNAs. We now performed qPCR analysis to confirm the expression level of these miRNAs after PPARalpha activation and in the tumors induced by DEN in $Myc^{F/F}$ and $Myc^{F/F;\ ERT2\text{-}Cre}$ mouse and found that there was a comparable expression of these miRNAs upon PPARalpha activation between $Myc^{F/F}$ and $Myc^{F/F;\ ERT2\text{-}Cre}$ mice. However, expression of the miR290-295 cluster was decreased in DEN-treated $Myc^{F/F;\ ERT2\text{-}Cre}$ liver. These data support the previous publication by Cairo et al., that miR-371-3 could be a direct target of MYC in HCC. We added these data to Figure 3C and Figure 4G.

Response to Reviewer 2

Major comments:

Reviewer #2: This is a focused manuscript that helps filling a gap in our understanding of the role of Myc in hepatocyte proliferation and carcinogenesis. They have used an elegant model that allowed an efficient hepatocyte-specific knock-down of Myc expression.

Comments

1. It would be nice showing that Myc is still down at the time of sacrifice of animals after 9 months. Also, what happens in the preneoplastic foci and adenomas? Are they derived from residual myc-positive cells?

Response: We added the data of genomic DNA recombination to Figure 4G. These data suggest that the DEN-induced tumor hepatocytes could escape Myc disruption by unknown mechanisms; this could explain that a small proportion of tumors developed in $Myc^{F/F;\ ERT2\text{-}Cre}$ mice.

2. Figure 2: I am somehow surprised by the high value of the labeling index on non-parenchymal cells in basal conditions. Please comment and also explain how labeling indexes were calculated (automated vs manual counting etc.).

Response: Non-parenchymal liver cells include Kupffer cells, sinusoidal endothelial cells, stellate cells and liver-associated lymphocytes. We think that renewal of sinusoidal endothelial cells and other non-parenchymal cells exist under basal conditions. Non-parenchymal cells also proliferate, interact with hepatocytes and contribute to hepatocyte proliferation upon proliferative stimuli, such as PPARalpha agonist and partial hepatectomy. This is supported by publications both from our group (Qu et al, Toxicol Sci, 2010) and others (Malik et al, Seminars in Cell and Developmental Biology, 2002). We counted the labeling index of non-parenchymal cells as follows: Images from five randomized microscopic fields (200X) were taken and numbers of BrdU positive non-parenchymal cells and total non-parenchymal cells were counted manually in a blind manner. The mean percentage of BrdU positive non-parenchymal cells was the labeling index for one mouse. Six to eight mice were included per group.

3. Results in Figs 4A, B, C and D should be analyzed with appropriate statistical tests.

Response: We added with statistical tests as shown in Figure 4A-D.

4. Table 1: why are there two p values on every line?

Response: The p values shown in every line were a range of p values for genes that significantly contributed to each biological function (from the lowest to the highest value). Please see the further explanation below.

5. Table 2: explain how the score was calculated.

Response: The score was calculated by Ingenuity Pathway Analysis software. The list of genes was overlaid onto a global molecular network developed from information contained in the IPA knowledge base (IPKB). For network analysis, IPA computed a score [p-score=−log10 (p-value)] according to the fit of the set of supplied genes and a list of biological functions stored in the IPKB. The score takes into account the number of genes in the network and the size of the network to approximate how relevant this network is to the original list of genes and allows the networks to be prioritized for further studies. A score >3 (p<0.001) indicates a >99.9% confidence that a gene network was not generated by chance alone. The network identified is presented as a graph indicating the molecular relationships between genes/gene products. Moreover, networks are preferentially enriched for genes with the most extensive interactions, and for which interactions are specific with the other genes in the network, rather than genes that are promiscuous and interact with a broad selection of genes throughout IPKB. The functional analysis identified the biological functions and the canonical signaling pathways that were most significant to the input data set. The significance of the association between the input data set and the functions or pathways was determined based on two parameters: (1) a ratio of the number of genes from the data set that map to the function/pathway divided by the total number of genes that map to the function/pathway and (2) a P-value calculated using Fischer's exact test determining the probability that the association between the genes in the dataset and the function/pathway is explained by chance alone. This was added to the legend to Table 2.

6. On page 12, it looks like the "unpublished data" (line 9) show the same thing than the results described just above (lines 5-8). This part should be rewritten.

Response: We rewrote this part on Page 12.

7. Final Words about Correspondence

Finally, it is very important to remember that the form of the text communicates to the reader as much as the content. Standard syntax, spelling, spacing and punctuation must be used for the correspondence to have its intended effect on the recipient, so before sending the text make sure to read it over several times.

8. Key Points

- For successful correspondence, preserving the relationship between the writer and reader should take top priority.
- Relationships are preserved with appropriate and unassuming language, especially when a request is being made.
- When replying to reviewers it is important to avoid projecting a defensive attitude.

9. Revision Exercise

Direction: Change the following letter so that it would be appropriate for a student to send to a professor.

Bob:

I have to be a little late for our meeting tomorrow; maybe 30 to 45 minutes. Let me know if it will be a problem.

Tom

Part II
Function, Structure and Meaning: The Organization of a Research Paper

Many of the writing choices made by native speakers are intuitive choices based on feeling rather than deliberate thought. However, that does not mean that this is the only way or even the best way to write well. Many foreign language writers may not have fully developed this intuition for the language, but these choices can also be based on conscious reasoning. An understanding of the concepts of structure, function and meaning can serve as the foundation of this reasoning process.

In the following chapters, the relationship between structure, function and meaning is used to help clarify why certain writing choices may be better than others may. Chapter Six surveys the basic organization of several commonly written research papers and chapters Seven through Thirteen provide further details section by section. The final chapter tries to illuminate some of the special difficulties encountered by writers whose first language is not English.

Chapter Six Types of Papers

Key Concepts

Hypothesis　　Independent variable　　Dependent variable

Papers written for medical journals vary widely in scope and purpose; however, it may be helpful to classify them in one of two categories: topic-based papers and hypothesis-based papers. A topic-based paper can be thought of as a general to particular analysis of a topic that is of interest to the medical community whereas a hypothesis-based paper begins with a question in need of an answer and then attempts to find and generalize that answer. Both types attempt to uncover new knowledge, however the methods differ and thus the structures of the papers will differ.

1. Topic Based Paper

1.1 Literature Review

A literature review can be thought of as an evaluation of the present state of knowledge on a topic of interest. The introduction should concisely provide enough background to understand the present state of knowledge concerning the topic, and to understand the importance of the topic. The introduction should be followed by a review of the most important or current research on the topic. The review should be divided into discreet subtopics as much as possible. The conclusion can be used to summarize and unify the subtopics; however, the conclusion should take one final step by clarifying the future direction of research based on the present situation. A typical structure of a literature review is as follows:

1) Abstract
2) Introduction
3) Topics
4) Conclusion

1.2 Case Report

A case report typically describes an unusual or unexpected occurrence within the presentation of a disease or a new method for treating a disease. The report should begin with an introduction followed by the description of the case. An account of how the case adds to the present state of medical knowledge including a relevant literature review should follow the case description. The report should end with a conclusion that concisely states the significance of the knowledge gleaned from the present case including recommendations and implications.

A typical structure of a case report is as follows:

1) Abstract

2) Introduction

3) Case description

4) Discussion

5) Conclusion

2. Hypothesis-based Paper

To better understand the structure and function of a hypothesis-based paper it is important to first understand the concept of independent and dependent variables. The difference between these two variables is based on the variable's position in a cause and effect relationship. If the variable is thought to be the cause within a relationship, it is independent. In other words, it is not dependent on another variable for any change that takes place. Whereas, if a variable is thought to be the result of or changed by another variable, it is then dependent on that variable for any change that takes place.

In Example 1, the independent variable is ***eating oranges*** and the dependent variable is ***intelligence***. The sentence claims that eating oranges causes a change in intelligence, not that intelligence causes a change in the eating of oranges. The entire sentence is a hypothesis. Notice how the hypothesis has been formed by linking the independent variable to the dependent variable with a precise verb that expresses the type of change that is thought to take place within the relationship.

Example 1

Eating oranges increases intelligence.

A hypothesis-based paper is a paper that tests the truth claims of a sentence or statement such as the hypothesis above. Moreover, the sentence or statement will include at least one independent variable, at least one dependent variable, and a precise verb that clearly expresses the type of change being proposed.

The standard hypothesis testing paper is divided into the following sections:

1) Title

2) Abstract

3) Introduction

4) Materials and Methods

5) Results

6) Discussion

The content and organization of the individual sections will be addressed in detail in the following chapters.

3. Key Points

- Papers written for medical journals can usually be classified as either topic based or hypothesis based.
- A topic-based paper is usually a description of a newly discovered process, method or material.
- A hypothesis-based paper usually tests the truth claims of a relationship between two or more independent and dependent variables.
- A hypothesis-based paper is usually divided into Five sections: abstract, introduction, methods and materials, results and discussion sections.

4. Revision Exercise

Direction: Revise the following hypothesis in order to allow the reader to differentiate between the independent and the dependent variables.

Lifestyle choices are associated with obesity.

Chapter Seven Title

Key Concepts

Phrase
Population
Message
Topic
Sentence

1. The Function of the Title

The function of the **TITLE** of a hypothesis testing paper is to express either the topic or the message of the paper through the independent variable and the dependent variable used in the study. For a descriptive paper, the function of the **Title** is also to express the topic or message; however, a descriptive paper has no independent variable so the topic or message is expressed through the dependent variable that the study describes. The population or material used should also be included in the **Title**. The function of the population in a **Title** is to set the minimum and maximum scope of effect for the study. The goal is to generalize the population as broadly as possible within the constraints of the study.

2. The Structure of the Title

2.1 Topic/Phrase Titles

The topic/phrase title is probably the most commonly used type of title. The topic of the paper tells what the paper is about and should be expressible by a noun phrase. It seems reasonable that the topic of a study that hypothesizes that eating oranges increases the intelligence of rats must be one of the three concepts (noun phrases) involved: ***eating oranges***, ***intelligence*** or ***rats***. However, this paper would not be about the independent variable, eating oranges, would not be about the dependent variable, intelligence, and would not be about the population, rats. The topic of the paper would be about the relationship between these three things.

Example 1 seems to meet the requirements of a topic/phrase title. It is a noun phrase that expresses the topic of the paper; however, if it were used as the title the reader would not be able to differentiate between the three concepts within the relationship. Intelligent rats may eat oranges or rats that eat oranges may become more intelligent. In fact, it is not very clear how rats fit into the relationship. Therefore, this title would not fulfill the function of a title, because the exact relationship between the three concepts has not been explained clearly.

Example 1

The Relationship of Eating Oranges, Intelligence and Rats

By isolating the population from the other two concepts through prepositional phrases as in Example 2, it becomes clear that the concept ***rats*** is the population. However, it is still impossible to differentiate between an independent and a dependent variable. One more change is needed.

Example 2

The Relationship *between* Eating Oranges and Intelligence *in Rats*

Changing the title to Example 3, clearly expresses that eating oranges is the independent variable, intelligence is the dependent variable, and rats are the population. The problem with Examples 1 and 2 is that the noun ***relationship*** does not express a cause and effect, whereas the noun ***effect*** in Example 3 does. The title expresses the topic of the paper. It also expresses the function of each of the three concepts involved. In addition, the title is able to do these things within a noun phrase.

Example 3

The Effect of Eating Oranges on Intelligence in Rats

2.2 Message Phrase Titles

A topic title answers the question, "What is the paper about?" A message title answers the question, "What does the paper discover about the topic?" So to change Example 3 into a message title, the specific ***effect*** must be expressed. Three specific effects could be imagined: no change, increased intelligence or decreased intelligence. Three possible message titles could thus be imagined (Examples 4–6). The message is created by placing an adjective that expresses the effect in front of the dependent variable. The independent variable and population are each placed in prepositional phrases that follow the dependent variable. The title remains as a noun phrase.

Example 4

Unaffected Intelligence by Eating Oranges in Rats

Example 5

Increased Intelligence by Eating Oranges in Rats

Example 6

Decreased Intelligence by Eating Oranges in Rats

2.3 Message sentence Titles

English sentences must have a subject and a verb. To change a message phrase title into a sentence title, place the independent variable in the subject position and determine what verb best describes the change that takes place to the dependent variable. The dependent variable becomes the object of the verb and the population follows in a prepositional phrase (Examples 7–9).

Example 7

Eating Oranges does not Increase Intelligence in Rats

Example 8

Eating Oranges Increases Intelligence in Rats

Example 9

Eating Oranges Decreases Intelligence in Rats

The verb used in the title must be in the present tense. The reason for this is quite simple;

the title is not a description of the result of the study; it is a truth claim about a relationship. By changing to the past tense (Example 10), the title becomes a mere description of a one-time event that may or may not be true about the present. It no longer expresses a generalizable finding and no longer has value beyond the study.

Example 10

Eating Oranges Decreased Intelligence in Rats

3. Choosing a Title

The three titles already discussed fall on a continuum from the least to the most powerful. The topic/phrase title has the least power, but it is the most commonly used title. Usually, message/ phrase titles are reserved for surprising findings, when the message itself is unexpected and will have impact. In addition, sentence/message titles should usually be reserved for surprising and significant findings.

Finally, the positions of the variables can be changed to change the emphasis of a title. For instance, by rearranging the variables in Example 3 the emphasis can be switched from the independent variable to the dependent variable (Example 11). Emphasis should be placed on the variable that is most important to the intended readers. Example 3 would probably be the best if the intended readers were nutritionists, and Example 11 would probably be the best if the intended readers were cognitive psychologists.

Example 11

The Effect on Intelligence of Eating Oranges in Rats

4. Case Analysis

4.1 Being Informative and Complete

An informative and complete title should include the sufficient and necessary information for reader to know either what the research is about or what the research has discovered; Use study keywords and key terms; Inform readers about independent variable, dependent variable, observed effects, and study population.

Case 1

Effects of Intensive Diet and Exercise on Knee Joint Loads, Inflammation, and Clinical Outcomes among Overweight and Obese Adults with Knee Osteoarthritis: The IDEA Randomized Clinical Trial

The title provides the sufficient and necessary information of the research paper. The independent variables "***intensive diet and exercise***", dependent variables "***Knee Joint Loads, Inflammation, and Clinical Outcomes***" and the exact population "***Overweight and Obese Adults with Knee Osteoarthritis***" are all included in the title. The preposition ***with*** is used to precisely define the "***overweight and obese adults***". The methods of the research are provided in the subtitle "The IDEA Randomized Clinical Trial". The key words and terms of the paper are included in this title.

Case 2

Effect of a Behavioral Intervention to Increase Vegetable Consumption on Cancer Progression among Men with Early-Stage Prostate Cancer: The MEAL Randomized Clinical Trial

Similar in this title, sufficient and complete information is provided. The infinitive phrase ***to increase*** is used to provide the purpose of ***a Behavioral Intervention***. The preposition ***with*** is used to define the ***Men*** who are included in the research. All key terms are included in the title.

4.2 Being Accurate

Titles need to be comprehensible and enticing to a potential reader quickly scanning a table of contents or performing an online search, while at the same time not being as general or vague as to obscure what the paper is about. The proper use of prepositions is helpful to make the titles accurate and clear.

A preposition is a word or a group of words used before a noun, pronoun, or noun phrase to show direction, time, place, location, spatial relationships, or to introduce an object. Proper use of prepositions makes the title clearer and helps the reader to understand how the title elements are related to each other. Usually, ***in*** is used in front of the disease, purpose, place, or population (Case 3 to Case 8). Other typical prepositions used in the title are, ***for*** (referring to a purpose), ***with*** (referring to having), ***of*** (belonging to or regrading), and ***among*** (referring to more than two) etc.

(Case 9 to Case 15)

Case 3

Effect of High-Dose vs Standard-Dose Wintertime Vitamin D Supplementation on Viral Upper Respiratory Tract Infections **in** Young Healthy Children

Case 4

Effect of a Home-Based Exercise Intervention of Wearable Technology and Telephone Coaching on Walking Performance **in** Peripheral Artery Disease: The HONOR and Randomized Clinical Trial

Case 5

Montelukast and Fluticasone Compared with Salmeterol and Fluticasone **in** Protecting against Asthma Exacerbation in Adults: One Year, Double Blind, Randomised, Comparative Trial

Case 6

Long-term developmental effects of withholding parenteral nutrition for 1 week **in** the pediatric intensive care unit: a 2-year follow-up of the PEPanic international, randomized, controlled trial

Case 7

Multidisciplinary diabetes care with and without bariatric surgery **in** overweight people: a randomized controlled trial

Case 8

Management of Coronary Disease **in** Patients with Advanced Kidney Disease

Case 9

Initial Invasive or Conservative Strategy **for** Stable Coronary Disease

Case 10

Risk of Developing Type 2 Diabetes in Individuals **with** a Psychiatric Disorder: A Nationwide

Register-Based Cohort Study

Case 11

Dolutegravir dosing for children **with** HIV weighing less than 20 kg: pharmacokinetic and safety sub-studies nested in the open-label, multicenter, randomized, non-inferiority ODYSSEY trial

Case 12

Clinical and cost effectiveness **of** mobile phone supported self-monitoring of asthma: multicenter randomized controlled trial

Case 13

Effect **of** Continuous Glucose Monitoring on Hypoglycemia in Older Adults with Type1 Diabetes: A Randomized Clinical Trial

Case 14

Effect of Acupuncture vs Sham Acupuncture or Waitlist Control on Joint Pain Related to Aromatase Inhibitors **among** Women with Early-Stage Breast Cancer

Case 15

Effect of Ramipril on Walking Times and Quality of Life **among** Patients with Peripheral Artery Disease and Intermittent Claudication: a Randomized Controlled Trial

4.3 Being Brief

Brevity means the minimum words are used to provide the sufficient information of the research paper. A better way to make titles brief is by omitting unnecessary words, mostly, omitting the article **the** in the titles (Case 16).

Case 16

The Effect of Laparoscopic vs Open Distal Gastrectomy on 3-Year Disease-Free Survival in Patients with Locally Advanced Gastric Cancer: The CLASS-01 Randomized Clinical Trial

(Note: **the** was finally omitted in the published version.)

Usually, words like ***studies of/on*** are not placed at the beginning of a title. That is because these words, like ***a research on, investigations on*** and ***a study on***, give no specific information and can be omitted to make the title briefer. Nevertheless, there is an exception. Look at Case 17.

Case 17

ARTIST (osteoarthritis intervention standardized) **study** of standardized consultation versus usual care for patients with osteoarthritis of the knee in primary care in France: pragmatic randomized controlled trial

The words ***study of*** are placed at the beginning of this title (Case 17), because ***ARTIST*** is used to modify ***study*** which indicates the research focus and the key information. Thus, ***study of*** cannot be omitted.

5. Key Points

- The function of the title of a hypothesis-based paper is to present either the topic or the message of the paper through the independent and dependent variables.
- Most titles for hypothesis testing papers will present only the topic of the paper through a noun phrase.
- Titles that express the message of the paper can be written as either a phrase or a sentence.
- Good titles are inseparable from the keywords as well as accurate and careful drafting process.
- Removing extra and unspecific words is helpful to keep the title unambiguous, memorable, captivating, and informative.

6. Revision Exercise

Direction: Do the following exercises according to the specific requirement.

1) The following three titles each need revision before being used for the study described

in Example 12.

① The Association between Exercise and Stroke Recurrence in First-time Stroke Patients

② Decreased the Recurrence of Stroke through Exercise in First-time Stroke Patients

③ Exercise Decreased the Recurrence of Stroke in 320 First-time Stroke Patients

Example 12

We hypothesized that exercise can reduce the recurrence of stroke in first-time stroke patients. The stroke-recurrence rate of 320 first-time stroke patients who took part in a supervised post-stroke exercise program was compared to the national average recurrence rate.

2) Please decide whether these titles indicate a topic or a message.

① HIV-1 Neutralizing Antibodies Induced by Native-Like Envelope Trimers

② A Dose-Response Crossover Iodine Balance Study to Determine Iodine Requirements in Early Infancy1, 2

③ Measuring the Quality of Outpatient Treatment for Schizophrenia

④ Quantifying the Burden of Stillbirths Before 28 Weeks of Completed Gestational Age in High-Income Countries

⑤ A Bivalent Virus-Like Particle Based Vaccine Induces A Balanced Antibody Response Against Both Enterovirus 71 and Norovirus in Mice

3) Please revise the following titles according to what you have learnt.

① Test results and clinical significance of the four serum markers in health persons and others suffering with chronic hepatitis

② A Systematic, Multinational, Large-Scale Analysis on Comprehensive Comparative Effectiveness and Safety of First-Line Antihypertensive Drug Classes

③ A Study on Unstable Angina and Non-ST Segment Elevation Myocardial Infarction in Acute Coronary Syndrome

④ Nerve growth factor and neuronal apoptosis after spinal cord injury in rats

⑤ Treatment of Acute Hepatic Failure by Liver Transplantation

⑥ An Analysis of 38 Cases on Clinical Diagnosis of Primary Ureteral Carcinoma

⑦ Content of the paper: The research is about the prevalence of psychiatric disorders in adults. After comparing the data from rural and urban areas in China, you found the number in rural areas is much higher than that in the urban area.

Title: psychiatric disorders: rural and urban comparison

⑧ Ccntent of the paper: The research is about the meditation and nursing, and the researcher used quantitative study to find out how meditation makes nurses better communicators.

Title: How Mindful Nurses Make the Best Communicators

Chapter Eight Introduction

Key Concepts

Background	Hypothesis
The unknown	Signal phrase
Gap	Experimental approach

1. The Function of the Introduction Section

INTRODUCTION, called "background" in some journals, lays the foundation for the research paper. It may be described as the gate to a city. It may also resemble a mental roadmap that should explain "the known", "the unknown", and the new knowledge added by the findings of the current research.

Introduction presents the background information to convince the readers of the importance of data added to the field. In addition, it sets the scene for readers and paves the way for what is to follow. Of course, different journals have different requirement for the ***Introduction***, so ***Introduction Section*** should be tailored to the targeted journal.

Introduction has two functions. One is to provide enough information for the readers to understand the paper and the other is to arouse their interest in continuing reading the paper. A good introduction will help the writer sell the paper to a journal with high IF.

2. The Structure of the Introduction Section

The structure of the introduction is somewhat different from other sections of the paper, because the focus of this section (the hypothesis/approach) is placed at the end rather than at the beginning of this section:

1) Background

2) Unknown

3) Hypothesis (optional: Experimental Approach)

2.1 The Background

The **Introduction** starts with a short explanation of the background. The background will not include everything that is known about the subject, because its specific function is to provide only the information necessary for understanding the hypothesis, and for understanding what led to the hypothesis. The hypothesis can be thought of as the border between what is known and what is unknown about a subject. The background is what the readers need to know to cross that border.

In a paper titled ***"The Effect of Eating Oranges on Intelligence in Rats",*** the background should show what led to the belief that a link exists between these two variables. For instance, if it were known that eating oranges increases blood flow to certain areas of the brain, then this information would imply that the hypothesis could be true, and would lead to the hypothesis.

Usually it is too abrupt to move directly from the background to the hypothesis, so between these two essential elements, it is a good practice to place a transition sentence about what is still unknown, to lead up to the hypothesis.

2.2 The Unknown

The **Unknown** functions as a transition from the background to the hypothesis. It should be one sentence that shows that the research question or hypothesis is the next logical step. In the ***Effect of Eating Oranges on Intelligence in Rats*** study, the known to unknown transition would look something like Example 1. Notice how the border between what is known and what is unknown has been crossed, but the hypothesis has not been proposed. The reader has been brought to the hypothesis, is anticipating the hypothesis and has the necessary information for understanding the hypothesis.

Example 1

It is known that citrus fruit increases blood flow to the brains of some mammals. However, it is unknown whether this increased blood flow results in greater cognitive ability.

2.3 The Hypothesis

The **Hypothesis** is the focal point of the introduction. At this point, the reader is told exactly what will be revealed by the study. The title clearly expresses the independent variable, the dependent variable and the population. The introduction must do more than this. In the example above, it would not be enough to know that a change in intelligence will be measured; it needs to be clear what type of change in intelligence will be measured. In the example, the type of change that will be measured is an increase, so the verb ***increase*** must be included in the hypothesis (Example 2).

Example 2

Eating oranges increases intelligence in rats.

Some verbs may express that a change takes place without expressing the type of change. These types of verbs should be avoided in the hypothesis. For example, Example 3 fulfills the function of a sentence title because the relationship of the variables has been made clear; however, it does not fulfill the function of a hypothesis because the type of change has not expressed. It is not immediately clear how a researcher could measure an effect (Example 3); however, it is clear that an increase could be measured (Example 2). The four essential elements in the hypothesis are the independent and dependent variables, the population and the type of change that will be measured.

Example 3

Eating oranges affects intelligence in rats.

The verb in the hypothesis must be in the present tense for the same reason that the verb in a message/sentence title must be in the present tense. The present tense indicates that the claim is not restricted to the present study. It is generalizable to any situation in which the independent variable encounters the dependent variable in the stipulated population and conditions.

By using both variables and a present tense verb that expresses the type of change that will be measured, two types of hypothesis clauses can be written. Example 4 is a standard hypothesis and Example 5 is a hypothesis with a question word. Both clauses are acceptable and both clauses must be preceded by an appropriate signal phrase.

Example 4

...eating oranges increases intelligence in rats.

Example 5

...whether eating oranges increases intelligence in rats.

2.4 Signal Phrases

A signal phrase is a phrase that lets the reader know what will come next. By convention, research papers follow a very strict order of topics and subtopics, so readers expect to be given information in a certain way and at a certain location in the paper. Skillful writers follow these conventions, and signal which of the essential elements is coming next. In the **Introduction**, the background, the unknown and the hypothesis should all be preceded by signal phrases (Example 6).

Example 6

Element	Possible Signal Phrase
Background	It is known that...
Unknown	It is unknown that...
Standard hypothesis	This study was designed to test the hypothesis that...
	In this study we tested the hypothesis that...
With a question word	This study was designed to determine whether...
	In this study we determined whether...

With the background, the unknown, the hypothesis and the appropriate signal phrases a concise introduction can be written (Example 7).

Example 7

It is known that citrus fruit increases blood flow to the brain in some mammals; however, it is unknown whether this increased blood flow results in greater cognitive ability. This study was designed to test the hypothesis that eating oranges increases intelligence in rats.

2.5 Experimental Approach

One additional element that is often included in the **Introduction** is the experimental approach. The experimental approach is a very short explanation of how the hypothesis was tested. It should be included if it is not immediately clear to the reader how such an experiment could be designed. If included, the experimental approach should be very short, often included in the same sentence as the hypothesis. If it is included, it must have a signal phrase. However, if the experimental approach is placed in the same sentence as the hypothesis, one signal phrase can be used to signal both the hypothesis and the experimental approach. In Example 8 below the signal phrase (***to determine***) signals both the hypothesis, and the experimental approach. If the hypothesis is bare (no question word) a different signal phrase should be used (Example 9). Also, notice that the verb in the experimental approach is in the past tense (***compared***). Unlike the hypothesis, the experimental approach refers to a past and completed event.

Example 8

To determine whether eating oranges increases intelligence in rats, we compared the ability to solve a maze exit problem between an orange consumption group and a control group.

Example 9

To test the hypothesis that eating oranges increases intelligence in rats, we compared the ability to solve a maze exit problem between an orange consumption group and a control group.

One final decision to be made about the experimental approach involves **point of view**, which will be covered more carefully in the next chapter. The subject and the main verb used in Examples 8 and 9 (***we compared***) create a first-person-plural point of view that emphasizes the action of the study, what ***we*** did. The point of view can be changed to emphasize either the independent variable (Example 10) or the dependent variable (Example 11) by using a passive voice verb to change the subject (Example 12).

Example 10

…an orange consumption group and a control group were compared by ability in the completion of a maze exit problem.

Example 11

…the ability to complete a maze exit problem was compared between an orange consumption group and a control group.

Example 12

Emphasis	**Subject**	**Main Verb**
Action	We	Active Voice
Dependent variable	Dependent Variable	Passive Voice
Independent variable	Independent Variable	Passive Voice

3. Case Analysis

1) Case 1

A. General Structure Analysis

Multidisciplinary diabetes care with and without bariatric surgery in overweight people: a randomised controlled trial

John M Wentworth, Julie Playfair, Cheryl Laurie, Matthew E Ritchie, Wendy A Brown, Paul Burton, Jonathan E Shaw, Paul E O'Brien

This paper is from www.thelancet.com/diabetes-endocrinology Vol 2 July 2014 (doi: 10.1016/S213-8587 (14)70066-X). Its **Introduction** is composed of four paragraphs, falling into three moves of the general structure of introduction.

The first move: the known

The Original Article	Comment	Features
Para. 1: Excess body weight is a dominant driver of type 2 diabetes, a disease that places a huge burden on individuals through reduced wellbeing and productivity, and on society through increased health costs. Management of type 2 diabetes is generally framed within a chronic disease model, with an expectation of progressive deterioration in glucose control over time.	The beginning two sentences present the general topic: *excessive body weight with type 2 diabetes and its difficult management*. Thus, the authors provide evidence for their study.	**Claim importance for the study**

continued

The Original Article	Comment	Features
This management approach has been investigated in randomized trials of lifestyle change or bariatric surgery, which show that weight loss in obese people with type 2 diabetes reduces drug burden and frequently achieves diabetes remission within 2 years.	This sentence provides statement about *the management approach in weight loss of obese people with type 2 diabetes in randomized trial of lifestyle change or bariatric surgery*. The Intervention for obese people with type 2 diabetes can reduce drug burden and later achieves better results within 2 years. It is effective.	**Narrow down the topic**

The second move: the unknown/the gap

The Original Article	Comment	Features
Para. 2: The effect of substantial weight loss on outcomes in overweight but not obese people (BMI between 25 and 30 kg/m^2) with type 2 diabetes is less well established. Investigators of the Look AHEAD trial showed that, after 1 year, modest weight loss of 8·6% bodyweight after lifestyle intervention was associated with a diabetes remission rate of roughly 10% in people whose starting BMI was less than 8.6% kg/m^2. Reports of the effect of bariatric surgery in overweight people with type 2 diabetes are limited to observational studies of gastric bypass, intestinal exclusion, or interposition surgery, and describe improved glycemic control after surgery but serious perioperative complications in up to 7% of patients. ***To date, no randomized trials of bariatric surgery in overweight but not obese people have been reported, and its true benefit, if any, remains uncertain.***	Para. 2 moves to *What is unknown*. That is there is no well-built evidence for how big weight loss can affect the overweight people with type 2 diabetes. The next two sentences further support this statement. One is the Look AHEAD trial result. The investigators found that only one year later after lifestyle intervention, even a mild weight loss, like 10%of bodyweight, could affect a diabetes remission rate, about 10% of people with BMI less than 32.5%. The other is the results from bariatric surgery in overweight people with type 2 diabetes could only be found in observational studies of some surgeries. The last sentence in this paragraph, *To date, no randomized trials of bariatric surgery in overweight but not obese people have been reported, and its true benefit, if any, remains uncertain* describes the gap in the present understanding of the effects of bariatric surgery on overweight but not obese people.	**The unknown and the gap**

continued

The Original Article	Comment	Features
Para. 3: Laparoscopic adjustable gastric banding is a common outpatient operation for obese people that has a favorable safety profile compared with other bariatric operations13, 14 and provides a durable effect, with substantial weight loss sustained for at least 15 years. Our previous randomized trial comparing laparoscopic adjustable gastric band surgery with medical weight management in moderately obese people with type 2 diabetes (BMI 30–40 kg/m²) showed that gastric banding induced diabetes remission more often than did medical therapy after 2 years of follow-up.	The first sentence in Para. 3 is the further explanation to Laparoscopic adjustable gastric banding, showing that this intervention applied for obese people is safe and effective. In addition, the second sentence is literature about previous randomized trial. These two sentences put together, reinforce the feasibility of the current study on the overweight people.	**Further introduction to the background**

The third move: the aim/hypothesis

The Original Article	Comment	Features
Para. 4: We did this trial to establish whether laparoscopic adjustable gastric banding had a similar effect on glucose control in people with type 2 diabetes who were overweight but not obese (BMI 25–30 kg/m²). We postulated that laparoscopic adjustable gastric banding in addition to multidisciplinary diabetes care would improve glycaemic control with acceptable comparative costs and safety compared with multidisciplinary care alone.	This last paragraph in Introduction section explains the aim of the current study and put forward the hypothesis. This lays foundation for the paper to move from the Introduction section to the next section—The Materials and Methods.	Clear statement of the **aim** and the **hypothesis** of the current study

B. The Language Features

- **The Tenses Used**

The Original Article	Comment
Para. 1: Excess body weight ***is*** a dominant driver of type 2 diabetes, a disease that ***places*** a huge burden on individuals through reduced wellbeing and productivity, and on society through increased health costs. Management of type 2 diabetes ***is generally framed*** within a chronic disease model, with an expectation of progressive deterioration in glucose control over time.	To describe the current state of knowledge of excess body of weight, **the present tense** is used in the first two sentences.

continued

The Original Article	Comment
Para. 1: This management approach ***has been investigated*** in randomized trials of lifestyle change or bariatric surgery, which ***show*** that weight loss in obese people with type 2 diabetes ***reduces*** drug burden and frequently achieves diabetes remission within 2 years.	To describe a process that began in the past and has not yet finished, **the present perfect tense** is used. **The present tense** is used to show the fact of research results.
Para. 2: The effect of substantial weight loss on outcomes in overweight but not obese people (BMI between 25 and 30 kg/m^2) with type 2 diabetes ***is*** less well established. Investigators of the Look AHEAD trial ***showed*** that, after 1 year, modest weight loss of 8.6% bodyweight after lifestyle intervention ***was associated with*** a diabetes remission rate of roughly 10% in people whose starting BMI ***was*** less than 32.5 kg/m^2. Reports of the effect of bariatric surgery in overweight people with type 2 diabetes ***are limited*** to observational studies of gastric bypass, intestinal exclusion, or interposition surgery, and ***describe*** improved glycaemic control after surgery but serious perioperative complications in up to 7% of patients. To date, no randomized trials of bariatric surgery in overweight but not obese people ***have been reported***, and its true benefit, if any, ***remains*** uncertain.	In this paragraph, the first sentence is the **present tense** to show the statement is a fact: *is less established.* The second sentence describes a past trial, so the **past tense** is used: *Showed, be associated with, was.* When it comes to the current facts, the present tense is used: *are limited, describe, have been reported, remains.*
Para. 4: We ***did*** this trial to establish whether laparoscopic adjustable gastric banding ***had*** a similar effect on glucose control in people with type 2 diabetes who ***were*** overweight but not obese (BMI 25–30 kg/m^2). We ***postulated*** that laparoscopic adjustable gastric banding in addition to multidisciplinary diabetes care ***would improve*** glycaemic control with acceptable comparative costs and safety compared with multidisciplinary care alone.	This sentence is to formulate the author's objectives; the **past tense** is used: *did this trial, had, were.* When it comes to the hypothesis, the first verb (*postulate*) is past tense and the tense *would improve* is used for the verb in the clause.

- **Word Appreciation**

The Original Article	Comment
Sentence 1 from Para. 1: Management of type 2 diabetes is ***generally*** framed within a chronic disease model, with an expectation of progressive deterioration in glucose control over time.	Here the adverb *generally* is a good choice. It shows that the management of type 2 diabetes is commonly/universally/popularly treated as a chronic disease and this kind of treatment has been well accepted. According to the paper, this kind of treatment works well among the obese people with type 2 diabetes. Thus, this general treatment to type 2 diabetes lays a solid foundation for the further research among the overweight people with type 2 diabetes. Imagine the meaning of the sentence without this adverb.

continued

The Original Article	Comment
Sentence 2 from Para. 2: The effect of substantial weight loss on outcomes in overweight but not obese people (BMI between 25 and 30 kg/m^2) with type 2 diabetes is ***less well established***.	*well established* means well-known or validated. When we say that something is well-established, we mean that it has been in existence for quite a long time and is successful. According to the paper, evidences for how well substantial weight loss could affect overweight with type 2 diabetes are insufficient. The word "*LESS*" indicates that the authors are less than 100-percent certain, but confident enough and signals how well they balance caution and confidence in their research. Think if the sentence goes like this: The effect of substantial weight loss on outcomes in overweight but not obese people (BMI between 25 and 30 kg/m^2) with type 2 diabetes is *NOT* well established. *Not well established* makes the sentence sound more aggressive. In most academic writing, it is better to avoid being too much assertive.

2) Case 2

A. General Structure Analysis

JAMA Cardiology | Original Investigation

Vitamin D Supplementation and Cardiovascular Disease Risks in More Than 83 000 Individuals in 21 Randomized Clinical Trials
A Meta-analysis

This paper is from https: //jamanetwork.com/by a University of Rochester User on 07/20/2019. The **Introduction** in this paper is composed of two paragraphs, falling into three moves of the general structure of introduction. The first paragraph is the first move, that is what is known and the second paragraph can be divided into two moves, that is, the unknown/gap and the experimental approach.

The first move: the known

<table>
<tr><th>The Original Article</th><th>Comment</th><th>Features</th></tr>
<tr><td rowspan="2">Para. 1:
Observational studies have suggested an inverse association between serum 25-hydroxyvitamin D levels and risk of cardiovascular disease (CVD) events. Specifically, low vitamin D levels have been linked to an increased risk of myocardial infarction (MI), stroke, CVD mortality, and heart failure in case-control and other prospective epidemiologic studies. Additionally, vitamin D receptors are expressed in vascular tissues, including the myocardium and vascular smooth muscle, directly influencing calcium influx, muscle relaxation, and diastolic function. Vitamin D also has effects on the renin-angiotensin-aldosterone system and parathyroid hormone and may influence endothelial function and arterial thrombogenesis.</td><td>The first sentence presents the general topic of this paragraph. Observational studies have reported an association between low serum vitamin D levels and elevated risk of cardiovascular disease events.</td><td>Claim importance for the study</td></tr>
<tr><td>The next three sentences provide evidence for their topic. Thus, the authors provide enough background information and set the context for this article.</td><td>Narrow down the topic</td></tr>
</table>

The second move and the third move: the unknown and the experimental approach

The Original Article	Comment	Features
Para. 2: Vitamin D level supplementation has increased in primary care settings in the United States. Assessment of vitamin D supplementation for cardiovascular disease prevention has been a subject of growing interest in recent randomized clinical trials (RCTs). Owing to insufficient data regarding cardiovascular benefits of screening and treatment of asymptomatic low vitamin D in adults, the US Preventive Services Task Force has not recommended vitamin D supplementation to prevent cardiovascular disease (via I statement, which indicates insufficient evidence).	Although Vitamin D level supplementation has increased in primary care settings in the US, there is still no clear statement to prove the causation of vitamin D supplementation in reducing major adverse cardiovascular events because of possible unmeasured confounding.	**What is unknown**
Although previous randomized clinical trials assessing vitamin D supplementation and cardiovascular disease have been limited and inconclusive, several recent large-scale trials have added substantial data to the evidence base. Therefore, we conducted a meta-analysis of all RCTs to date that evaluate the efficacy of vitamin D supplementation in the prevention of cardiovascular disease.	The previous randomized clinical trials are limited and inconclusive in the assessment of vitamin D supplementation and cardiovascular disease events, but several recent large-scale trials provide plenty of data for the assessment. Therefore the authors conducted a meta-analysis of all RCTs they could collect to evaluate the causation between vitamin D supplementation and the prevention of cardiovascular disease.	**What is the experimental approach and what was done**

B. Language Features

- **The Tenses Used**

Original Article	Comment
Para. 1: Observational studies ***have suggested*** an inverse association between serum 25-hydroxyvitamin D levels and risk of cardiovascular disease (CVD) events. Specifically, low vitamin D levels ***have been linked to*** an increased risk of myocardial infarction (MI), stroke, CVD mortality, and heart failure in case-control and other prospective epidemiologic studies. Additionally, vitamin D receptors ***are expressed*** in vascular tissues, including the myocardium and vascular smooth muscle, directly influencing calcium influx, muscle relaxation, and diastolic function. Vitamin D also ***has effects*** on the renin-angiotensin-aldosterone system and parathyroid hormone and ***may influence*** endothelial function and arterial thrombogenesis. **Para. 2:** Vitamin D level supplementation ***has increased*** in primary care settings in the United States. Assessment of vitamin D supplementation for cardiovascular disease prevention ***has been*** a subject of growing interest in recent randomized clinical trials (RCTs). Owing to insufficient data regarding cardiovascular benefits of screening and treatment of asymptomatic low vitamin D in adults, the US Preventive Services Task Force ***has not recommended*** vitamin D supplementation to prevent cardiovascular disease (via I statement, which indicates insufficient evidence). Although previous randomized clinical trials assessing vitamin D supplementation and cardiovascular disease ***have been limited and inconclusive***, several recent large-scale trials ***have added*** substantial data to the evidence base. Therefore, we ***conducted*** a meta-analysis of all RCTs to date that evaluate the efficacy of vita-min D supplementation in the prevention of cardiovascular disease.	To show that the studies began sometime in the past, and is not yet complete, *present perfect* tense is used: *have suggested, have been linked to, has increased, has been, have not been recommended* To show the facts, *present tense* is used: *are expressed, has effects, may influence.* To formulate the objective, *past tense* is used: *conducted*

- **Word Appreciation**

Original Article	Comment
Para. 1: Observational studies have suggested an inverse association between serum 25-hydroxyvitamin D levels and risk of cardiovascular disease (CVD) events. ***Specifically,*** low vitamin D levels have been linked to an increased risk of myocardial infarction (MI), stroke, CVD mortality, and heart failure in case-control and other prospective epidemiologic studies. ***Additionally***, vitamin D receptors are expressed in vascular tissues, including the myocardium and vascular smooth muscle, directly influencing calcium influx, muscle relaxation, and diastolic function. Vitamin D ***also*** has effects on the renin-angiotensin-aldosterone system and parathyroid hormone and may influence endothelial function and arterial thrombogenesis.	In this paragraph, the authors use the adverb *specifically* to induce the citation of the first group of literature to support the topic sentence. *Additionally* at the beginning of the next sentence links similar facts. *Also* in the next sentence placed before the verb *has*. These three adverbs connect the three sentences and produce a logical and clear context for the topic.

Common adverbs used for different effects

Effects	Adverbs
Link similar facts or related ideas	similarly; additionally; moreover; furthermore; in addition
Move between two different ideas or results that don't agree	however; in contrast; conversely
Indicate the order or timing of events and discoveries	initially; recently; subsequently; finally
Indicate the order of the experimental methods and results	initially; firstly; secondly; subsequently; next; finally; lastly
Link two sentences or sections of the paper	hence; consequently; accordingly; therefore; since; as

4. Key Points

- The function of the introduction of a hypothesis-based paper is to present the hypothesis.
- A standard introduction will follow the conventional order of elements: the background and the unknown followed by the sentence containing the hypothesis, with an optional experimental approach.
- It is very important to choose a specific and clear present-tense verb for linking the independent variable to the dependent variable in the sentence containing the hypothesis.
- It is important to use signal phrases or clauses at the beginnings of the sentences that mark a shift between the background, unknown and hypothesis.

5. Revision Exercise

Direction: The following Introduction needs revision before being used. Read it and answer the following questions and then revise it.

Drinking one to two cups of coffee per day can protect against some cardiovascular diseases. Can coffee restore Cognitive Function? To determine whether coffee can restore cognitive function in Alzheimer patients, a group of age and disease matched participants were divided into a study group and a control group, in which the study group was given 2 cups of coffee per day and the control group was given a coffee substitute consisting mainly of barley. Cognitive Function was tested before and after the study for comparison.

1) Which section of a research paper would include this paragraph?

2) Independent Variable (s):

3) Dependent Variable (s):

4) Population:

5) Writing mechanics problem:

6) Revise the sentence containing the unknown:

7) Point out one change that you would make to the 1st sentence:

8) Write a topic/phrase title for this paper:

Chapter Nine Materials and Methods

Key Concepts

Topic sentence
Subsections
Subtitles/subheadings
Point of view
Emphasis
Chronological order
Emphatic order
Parentheses

1. The Function of the Materials and Methods Section

MATERIALS and METHODS, commonly the second section of IMRaD formatted research paper, is a detailed and precise description of how the hypothesis was proven true or false, including all materials and procedures used. By reading this section, a trained researcher should be able to duplicate both the materials and methods and educated readers should have enough information to evaluate the efficacy of the methods used. This section must answer the following three questions:

1) What was used?

2) What was done?

3) How was it done?

2. The Structure of the Materials and Methods Section

The three core questions determine the generic structure of the Materials and Methods section, and the detailed answers to these three questions form its main content. The answers are usually organized by subsections.

2.1 The Organization of Subsections

Subtitles can be used to signal the transitions between and within the three questions (Example 1).

Example 1

Questions	Subtitles for Animal Studies	Subtitles for Clinical Studies
What was used?	• Materials • Animals	• Study Subjects • Inclusion Criteria • Exclusion Criteria
What was done?	• Preparation • Study Design or Protocol	• Study Design or Protocol
How was it done?	• Methods of Measurement • Calculations • Analysis of Data	• Methods of Measurement • Calculations • Analysis of Data

For this section, one thing to note is the guidelines and checklists provided by target journals. In ***The Lancet***, for example, its official website offers detailed information in "**Preparing your manuscript**" on what should be included in the methods section. Similarly, ***Journal of American Medical Association (JAMA)*** offers an "**Instructions for Authors**" on its official website. ***The New England Journal of Medicine (NEJM)*** puts this information in its "**Author Center**" and provides detailed guidelines for reporting experiment data. It is a good idea to refer to the authoritative information when organizing ideas.

2.2 The Organization within Subsections

Organization of the paragraphs within subsections and the details within the paragraphs should be in either chronological order or order of importance.

Chronological order means to follow a time order or a time pattern. A series of events or actions can be narrated according to the sequence in which they occur. The preparations subsection is usually written in chronological order.

Emphatic order means to follow an order of importance. The main points are organized in the sequence from the most to the least important. In the methods of measurement section, if both the independent and dependent variables have methods, the methods for the independent variables should be first. If there are only methods for the dependent variables, the variables that answer the research question should be first.

The emphasis of the study design will be determined by the **point of view** of the topic sentence. In Example 2, the dependent variable (*the ability to solve…was compared*) is emphasized. In Example 3, the first-person-plural point of view emphasizes the action or method used (*we compared the ability to solve…*) .

Example 2

To determine whether eating oranges increases intelligence in rats, the ability to solve a maze exit problem was compared between an orange consumption group and a non-consumption group.

Example 3

To determine whether eating oranges increases intelligence in rats, we compared the ability to solve a maze exit problem between an orange consumption group and a non-consumption group.

Either **point of view** could be defended as the best choice, but once the choice is made, the emphasis should remain consistent throughout the materials and methods section. If the emphasis of a variable is used (Example 2), many of the sentences that follow will be in passive voice. If the emphasis of the action is used (Example 3), many of the sentences will begin with the subject ***We***. Skillful authors are able to switch emphasis without disrupting the flow of the narrative, but if you are not sure of yourself, it is better to keep a consistent point of view and emphasis.

The specific organization within a subsection allows readers to be clear about the flow of ideas in a certain subsection. Still, it is necessary to ensure each paragraph within this subsection develops for one single topic. What helps is to begin each paragraph within a subsection with a topic sentence to announce the topic or the message of the paragraph. **Topic sentence** is also an efficient and effective way to achieve smooth transitions between paragraphs.

For **paragraphs concerning materials**, the topic sentence will introduce the topic of the paragraph, the material. For instance, in the ***Animals*** subsection, the first sentence of the first paragraph could be: *Male and female ICR mice were purchased from…* This sentence could be followed by details concerning the care and preparation of the mice.

For **paragraphs concerning methods**, the topic sentence should announce the message of the paragraph. In other words, the topic sentence should not only express the method, but also the reason for the method. This is often accomplished with an infinitive phrase (Example 4). The infinitive phrase functions to provide the purpose of the method that follows, which is the message of the paragraph.

Example 4

To measure the cognitive ability of both the experimental and control mice...

For **the study design**, a restatement of the hypothesis and experimental approach functions as the topic sentence (Example 5). This topic sentence expresses the message of the entire subsection. All paragraphs within the subsection will be related to this sentence. If only one paragraph is used, this topic sentence is sufficient; however, if more than one paragraph is needed, then each subsequent paragraph should have its own topic sentence.

Example 5

To determine whether eating oranges increases intelligence in rats, the ability to solve a maze exit problem was compared between an orange consumption group and a non-consumption group.

3. The Content of the Materials and Methods Section

To answer the three core questions in the Materials and Methods section, it is essential to include sufficient research information in each subsection. Such information, like detailed procedures, properties, reasons, calculations, etc. makes up the content of this section. The materials/study subjects answer the question "What was used?". The study design answers "What was done?". The methods of measurement plus data analysis answer "How was it done?".

3.1 Materials

For **drugs**, their generic name, manufacturer, purity, and concentration should be stated. It is also recommended to provide the amount of drug administered per kilogram of body weight and its duration.

For **human subjects/participants/patients**, the following five types of information should be included.

1) the target population, sample size and sampling method, sample representativeness, recruitment and randomization procedures;

2) the basic demographic profile: age, sex, race, height, weight, state of health or disease, specific medical and surgical management useful to researchers to compare data, or to clinicians who want to see if the findings are applicable to their patients;

3) the inclusion and exclusion criteria of the participants;

4) the research approval by appropriate committees, for example, an approval from the ethics committee with its registration number or a statement conducted according to some protocols, such as ***The Declaration of Helsinki.***

5) a statement about **informed consent or assent forms.**

3.2 Study Design

For hypothesis-testing research, since all the experiments are designed in advance, the overview of the experiments should be given in a separate subsection of the methods section—**study design**, also named in other ways in different journals, such as **trial design**, **trial oversight**, or **experimental design**. The study design of a clinical research commonly falls into one of the following five types:

1) randomized controlled trial (RCT);

2) prospective/retrospective cohort study;

3) case-control study;

4) cross-sectional survey;

5) non-randomized controlled trail(nRCT).

Authors can describe the type of research, for example, interventional study or observational study, longitudinal study or cross-sectional design. Besides, in the study design, such information is often included: research question (s), independent variables (interventions made), dependent variables (variables measured), all controls, baseline and control series (in some cases means placebo or sham experiments).

Furthermore, the study design should also make clear: components of one experiment, order and duration of the interventions (measurements and experiments), sample size (unless stated in other subsections like human subjects or data analysis).

There is possibly some overlap between the methods section and the introduction section, which helps to keep the storyline of the study running more smoothly. However, the study design in Materials and Methods is always more extensive than the experimental approach in Introduction, because the former includes more specific details, like timing and doses, which are not commonly included in the experimental approach in Introduction.

3.3 Method Description

As regards method description, it is worth noting how detailed the description should be as well as whether the reference should be given. For a well-known method, it does NOT need to be described, only with a reference provided. For a less well-known method, it needs stating its essential features and references. For a modified method, it needs describing its essential features of the modification as well as giving references. In addition, it is reasonable to give the purpose of the modification, if it would be helpful to readers. For a novel method, it needs a complete description so that potential readers can evaluate or employ this method with full understanding of how it works in future studies.

3.4 Data Analysis

When reporting the experimental data, the **calculation of data** will be first presented in the subsection of either "Methods of Measurement and Calculation" or "Statistical Analysis" where the derived variables were calculated. The second step is to summarize data. **Summary of data** includes information about both the magnitude of the data and variability. When the data appear to be drawn from a **normal distribution** (or, at least, are distributed symmetrically about the mean), it is reasonable to use the **mean** and **standard deviation** to summarize the data. The mean provides a description of the overall magnitude of the data and the standard deviation (SD) provides a measure of variability in the sample. When the data seem to come from a **skewed distribution** (that is, an inordinate number of high or low values, compared to the mean), the **median** and the **interquartile range** (the range between the 25th and the 75th percentiles) should be reported. The third step is to state **the statistical tests** used. For less well-known tests, it is only needed to give a reference (or a book that describes the tests used) to the report. However, for well-known tests, such as *t*-test, chi square, analysis of variance, linear regression, correlation, widely used nonparametric tests (for example, the Wilcoxon signed rank test), etc., the reference is not needed.

As regards the sample size, if the size analyzed for each comparison seems not obvious from the study design, the sample size (N) needs to be stated. In addition, the specific ***P* value** for differences of statistical significance is usually given in figure legends, footnotes to tables or results.

When ***P* value** is statistically significant but biologically or clinically unimportant, it is necessary to assess the size of difference compared with variability in the data sample through the calculation of **the 95% confidence interval**.

4. Case Analysis

4.1 Case 1

Case 1 is an article titled “COVID-19 mortality in patients with cancer on chemotherapy or other anticancer treatments: a prospective cohort study” published on *The Lancet* in 2020 on COVID-19 mortality in patients with cancer on chemotherapy or other anticancer treatments.

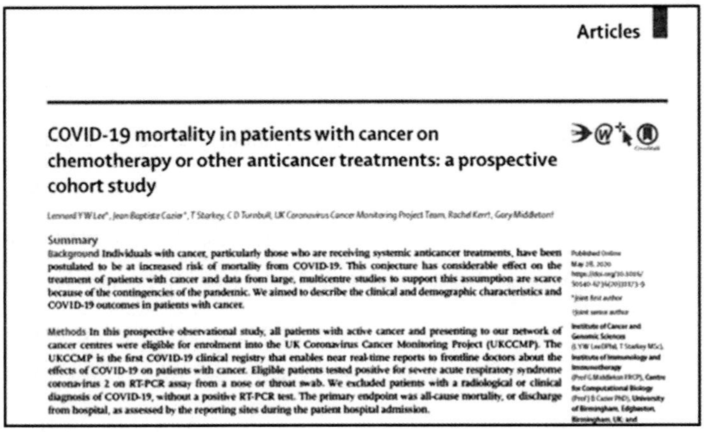

Articles

COVID-19 mortality in patients with cancer on chemotherapy or other anticancer treatments: a prospective cohort study

Lennard YW Lee*, Jean-Baptiste Cazier*, T Starkey, C D Turnbull, UK Coronavirus Cancer Monitoring Project Team, Rachel Kerr†, Gary Middleton†

Summary

Background Individuals with cancer, particularly those who are receiving systemic anticancer treatments, have been postulated to be at increased risk of mortality from COVID-19. This conjecture has considerable effect on the treatment of patients with cancer and data from large, multicentre studies to support this assumption are scarce because of the contingencies of the pandemic. We aimed to describe the clinical and demographic characteristics and COVID-19 outcomes in patients with cancer.

Methods In this prospective observational study, all patients with active cancer and presenting to our network of cancer centres were eligible for enrolment into the UK Coronavirus Cancer Monitoring Project (UKCCMP). The UKCCMP is the first COVID-19 clinical registry that enables near real-time reports to frontline doctors about the effects of COVID-19 on patients with cancer. Eligible patients tested positive for severe acute respiratory syndrome coronavirus 2 on RT-PCR assay from a nose or throat swab. We excluded patients with a radiological or clinical diagnosis of COVID-19, without a positive RT-PCR test. The primary endpoint was all-cause mortality, or discharge from hospital, as assessed by the reporting sites during the patient hospital admission.

Figure 1 The original article from The Lancet

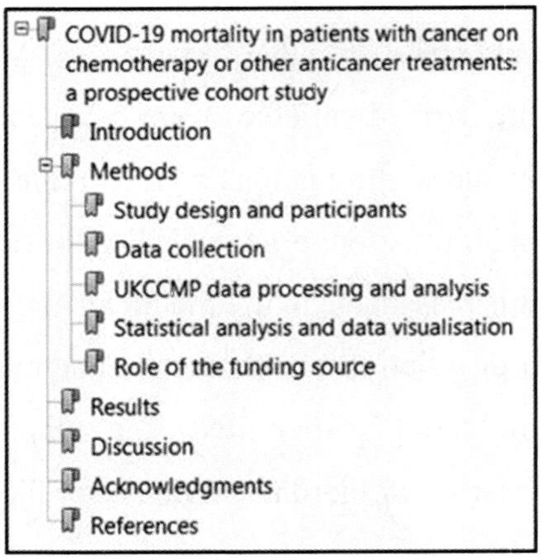

Figure 2 The overall organization

In the Introduction section, the research questions or the aims of the study are “to describe the clinical and demographic characteristics and COVID-19 outcomes in this cohort of patients with cancer and symptomatic COVID-19, and attempt to assess how the presence of cancer and the receipt of cytotoxic chemotherapy and other anticancer treatments affects the COVID-19 disease phenotype.”

A. The General Structure Analysis

The Structure of Methods

Subsections	**Description**	**Comment**
Subsection 1	Study Design and Participants	There are **3 paragraphs, answering "what was used".** **Para. 1** briefly describes the UK Coronavirus Cancer Monitoring Project (UKCCMP) database and states that this cohort study was approved by the appropriate committee at the institutional level. **Para. 2** explains the study subjects, the information about settings and time span as well as the inclusion and exclusion criteria. **Para. 3** categorizes stages of tumor and specifies the two kinds of participants: patients with cancer on chemotherapy and those with other anticancer treatments
Subsection 2	Data Collection	The paragraph in this section answers "**what was done and how was it done**". This paragraph describes how the prospective data collection was done, including data report, data entry and data assessment. It ends up with the criteria used for determining the COVID-19 severity category and the cancer type.
Subsection 3	UKCCMP Data Processing and Analysis	There are **2 paragraphs, continuing answering "what was done and how was it done"**. **Para. 1** introduces how the data were transferred through "the Compute and Storage for Life Science (CaStLeS)" at University of Birmingham. **Para. 2** describes how the data were curated and annotated.
Subsection 4	Statistical analysis and data visualization	The paragraph describes statistical methods with enough detail to afford a knowledgeable reader with access to the original data.
Subsection 5	Role of the funding source	This paragraph is required for reporting conflicts of interest. *The Lancet* provides online given format.

B. The Language Features

- **The Tenses Used**

The Materials and Methods section is generally written in the past tense, because it describes completed actions. An exception will be the verb used in the hypothesis of the topic sentence at the beginning of the study design and in current data processing and analysis. The verb used in these contexts is mostly in the present tense, as it was in the Introduction.

The Tenses Used

The Original Article	Comment
Data Collection: Prospective data collection was done by the pan-UK cancer centre emergency response network. Case reporting ***was led*** by a COVID-19 emergency response reporting individual (ERRI), supported by a local emergency response reporting group (LERRG) at each centre. The role of the LERRG ***was to ensure*** near continuous reporting of cases in situations of absence of the ERRI. The UKCCMP ***encouraged*** all local reporting sites to enter data in a real-time basis, as soon as a positive SARS-CoV-2 test ***had been identified***. The data fields ***were then updated*** as soon as treatment and outcomes ***had been identified*** and also to reflect the worse COVID-19 severity categories during hospitalisation. The ERRI ***was an oncologist*** who was trained or in training, who did data review, annotation, and entry. In a few centres, data entry ***was done*** by data managers but with direct oversight by the ERRI. All registry entries ***were de-identified*** at source to ensure data anonymity to researchers. Data ***was entered*** with the research electronic data capture (REDCap) application, an electronic data capture software system that is browser based and metadata driven. This secure electronic data capture platform ***is hosted*** by the Institute of Translational Medicine at the University of Birmingham, Birmingham, UK. Patient demographics, treatment details, COVID-19 disease course, and cancer features were obtained by the direct assessment of the ERRI and LERRG, or through hospital medical records. The COVID-19 severity category ***was determined*** according to WHO guidelines. Cancer type *was defined* according to the International Classification of Disease (10th revision) diagnostic codes.	To show that the studies began sometime in the past and is completed, ***the past tense*** is used: *was led, was to ensure, encouraged, had been identified, were then updated, was done, were de-identified, was entered ...*
Data Processing and Analysis: Within CaStLeS, the data ***are curated*** to avoid duplications and errors, then annotated with further information such as geolocation before they ***can be analysed and disseminated***. The deployment of an automatic work-flow system, with human interaction (human-in-the-loop), ***enables*** the delivery of near real-time robust data analytics to medical health professionals in oncology through a weekly report in addition to a secured interactive web portal. Importantly, CaStLeS ***enables*** delivery of national and local analytics with a dynamic level of granularity.	To show the current state of the data processing and analysis, ***the present tense*** is used, in contrast to the completed actions in data collection: *are curated, can be analysed and disseminated, enables.*

- **The Point of View and Voices**

The Original Article	Comment
Data Collection: Prospective data collection was done by the pan-UK cancer centre emergency response network. Case reporting ***was led*** by a COVID-19 emergency response reporting individual (ERRI), supported by a local emergency response reporting group (LERRG) at each centre. The role of the LERRG was to ensure near continuous reporting of cases in situations of absence of the ERRI. The UKCCMP encouraged all local reporting sites to enter data in a real-time basis, as soon as a positive SARS-CoV-2 test ***had been identified***. The data fields ***were then updated*** as soon as treatment and outcomes ***had been identified*** and also to reflect the worse COVID-19 severity categories during hospitalisation. The ERRI was an oncologist who was trained or in training, who did data review, annotation, and entry. In a few centres, data entry ***was done*** by data managers but with direct oversight by the ERRI. All registry entries ***were de-identified*** at source to ensure data anonymity to researchers. Data ***was entered*** with the research electronic data capture (REDCap) application, an electronic data capture software system that is browser based and metadata driven. This secure electronic data capture platform ***is hosted*** by the Institute of Translational Medicine at the University of Birmingham, Birmingham, UK. Patient demographics, treatment details, COVID-19 disease course, and cancer features were obtained by the direct assessment of the ERRI and LERRG, or through hospital medical records. The COVID-19 severity category ***was determined*** according to WHO guidelines. Cancer type *was defined* according to the International Classification of Disease (10th revision) diagnostic codes.	The Methods section mostly employs both points of the experiment and point of the experimenter (we). When it stresses the point of the experiment, the aspect of passive voice is generally used: *was led, had been identified, was then updated, was done, was de-identified, was entered, is hosted, was determined.* The use of the passive voice thus makes the topic, or the precise information prominent in the sentence. It also can help achieve objectivity and high consistency within this subsection or paragraph. It is the safest way for authors to develop sentences.
Statistical analysis and data visualization: ***We*** assessed whether the patient died or eventually achieved discharge, and observed the effect of anticancer treatment on outcomes.	When it stresses the point of the experimenter (we), the aspect of active voice is generally used: *We assessed...*

- **The Use of Parentheses**

Parentheses should be used for details that would otherwise break up the flow of the narrative. By using parentheses, these details are placed in the background so that they do not distract from the main message. The types of details that are often placed in parentheses include manufacturers' names, model numbers, weights, doses and concentrations.

The Original Article	Comment
Study design and participants: ...These patients were not part of a proactive surveillance programme. Patients with active cancer were defined as those with metastatic cancer, or on anticancer treatment in any setting ***(curative, radical, adjuvant, or neoadjuvant setting)*** or treated within the past 12 months with surgery cytotoxic chemotherapy, or radiotherapy.	Classified examples
Study design and participants: ...Stages of tumour were divided into those into primary tumour localised, which were localised to organ and therefore potentially resectable; primary tumour locally advanced, which had spread locally from the primary organ and was not resectable; metastatic, when there has been distant spread ***(stage IV)***; and patients in remission.	Specific clinical definitions or terms
Study design and participants: ...Patients were assessed by the local teams and review of their medical history as to whether they had received chemotherapy ***(which did not include treatment with denosumab)***, immunotherapy, hormonal therapies, or radiotherapy within 4 weeks of contraction of COVID-19.	Additional explanations
Data collection: ...Prospective data collection was done by the pan-UK cancer centre emergency response network. Case reporting was led by a COVID-19 emergency response reporting individual ***(ERRI)***, supported by a local emergency response reporting group ***(LERRG)*** at each centre.	Abbreviations
UKCCMP data processing and analysis: The data entered through REDCap was transferred securely through to the Compute and Storage for Life Science ***(CaStLeS)*** infrastructure as part of the Birmingham environment for academic research local cloud" at the Centre for Computational Biology, University of Birmingham.	Software names
Statistical analysis and data visualization: ...Multivariate analyses were done in SPSS ***(version 26.0.0.0)*** and Fisher's exact tests in R ***(version 3.6.3)***, using the fisher.	Version or release numbers

4.2 Case 2

Case 2 is an article titled "A Randomized, Controlled Trial of Liraglutide for Adolescents with Obesity" published on *The New England Journal of Medicine* in 2020.

The NEW ENGLAND JOURNAL of MEDICINE

ORIGINAL ARTICLE

A Randomized, Controlled Trial of Liraglutide for Adolescents with Obesity

Aaron S. Kelly, Ph.D., Pernille Auerbach, M.D., Ph.D., Margarita Barrientos-Perez, M.D., Inge Gies, M.D., Ph.D., Paula M. Hale, M.D., Claude Marcus, M.D., Ph.D., Lucy D. Mastrandrea, M.D., Ph.D., Nandana Prabhu, M.Sc., and Silva Arslanian, M.D., for the NN8022-4180 Trial Investigators*

ABSTRACT

BACKGROUND

Obesity is a chronic disease with limited treatment options in pediatric patients. Liraglutide may be useful for weight management in adolescents with obesity.

METHODS

In this randomized, double-blind trial, which consisted of a 56-week treatment period and a 26-week follow-up period, we enrolled adolescents (12 to <18 years of age) with obesity and a poor response to lifestyle therapy alone. Participants were randomly assigned (1:1) to receive either liraglutide (3.0 mg) or placebo sub-

From the Department of Pediatrics and Center for Pediatric Obesity Medicine, University of Minnesota Medical School, Minneapolis (A.S.K.); Novo Nordisk, Søborg, Denmark (P.A.); Pediatric Endocrinology, Hospital Ángeles Puebla, Puebla City, Mexico (M.B.-P.); the Department of Pediatrics, Division of Pediatric Endocrinology, Universitair Ziekenhuis Brussel, Brussels (I.G.); Novo Nordisk, Plainsboro,

In the Introduction section, the author states "In a previous study that involved adults with obesity or overweight who had either hypertension or dyslipidemia, liraglutide (3.0 mg) resulted in clinically meaningful weight loss and improvements in cardiometabolic markers and health–related quality of life. The present trial evaluated the efficacy and safety of subcutaneous liraglutide (3.0 mg) as an adjunct to lifestyle therapy for weight management in adolescents with obesity". The Methods section follows the generic structure and answers the three core questions (What was used? What was done? How was it done?) in four subsections with the corresponding subtitles:

- Trial Oversight
- Participants
- Trial Procedures and End Points
- Statistical Analysis

A. The General Structure Analysis

The Structure of Methods

Subsections	**Description**	**Comment**
Subsection 1	Trial Oversight	**Para. 1** starts with a generalized introduction of the trial design. It tells the study type, the author, sponsor and investigators' responsibilities. **Para. 2** describes a statement regarding obtaining approval from the ethics committee, a statement that the study was conducted according to the Declaration of Helsinki as well as the informed consent obtained from all participants before the initiation of any trial-related procedures.
Subsection 2	Participants	This only paragraph answers the question "**what was used**". It describes the inclusion and exclusion criteria for study subjects.
Subsection 3	Trial Procedures and End Points	There are **3 paragraphs, continuing answering "what was done and how was it done"**. **Para. 1** introduces what was done in a 12-week run-in period and how it was done in the different treatment to the liraglutide group and the volume-matched placebo group. **Para. 2** describes the primary end point about the change from baseline in the BMI standard-deviation score at week 56. **Para. 3** describes key safety end points. Para. 2 & 3 provide a complete list of end points.
Subsection 4	Statistical analysis	The only paragraph starts with the restatement of the hypothesis. Then it describes the calculation of the sample of 228 participants. Next, it analyzes the primary and secondary efficacy end points, the management of all the missing data, the additional analysis to the weight-related end points, assessment to the primary and continuous secondary efficacy end points. Finally, it mentions its exclusion of a provision of correction for multiplicity and its treatment to the results. This paragraph describes the process of the statistical analysis, enabling a knowledgeable reader with access to the original data.

B. The Language Features

- **The Tenses Used**

The Methods in this article mostly employ the simple past tense, describing completed actions. The exceptions (the present tense, the present perfect tense) can be found in the case of indicating more information in Appendix or necessary explanations for the widths of the confidence intervals.

The Tenses Used

The Original Article	Comment
Trial Oversight We ***conducted*** this randomized, double-blind, placebo-controlled, phase 3 trial from September 29, 2016, through August 8, 2019, at 32 sites in five countries. The trial ***had*** a 12-week run-in period, a 56-week treatment period (including dose escalation over a period of 4 to 8 weeks), and a 26-week follow-up period without treatment. The trial protocol with the statistical analysis plan ***is*** available at NEJM.org. The trial **was designed and overseen** by representatives of the trial sponsor (Novo Nordisk) with input from selected site investigators. The site investigators ***gathered*** the data, and the sponsor performed the data analyses. All the authors ***had*** full access to the data, ***directed and supervised*** the data analyses, ***interpreted*** the data, and vouch for the accuracy and completeness of the data and the fidelity of the trial to the protocol. The first author ***wrote*** the first draft of the manuscript with assistance from an independent medical writer funded by the sponsor. The manuscript ***was subsequently revised and approved*** by all the authors, who ***agreed*** to submit the manuscript for publication.	The past tense is employed when the article describes the complete actions: *conducted, had, was designed and overseen, gathered, directed and supervised, interpreted, wrote, was revised and approved, agreed.* When it describes a fact, the present tense is employed: *is available.*
Trial Procedures and End Points During the 12-week run-in period, all participants ***received*** lifestyle therapy, defined as counseling about healthy nutrition and physical activity for weight loss (further information ***is provided*** in the Supplementary Appendix). Participants who fulfilled the randomization criteria ***were randomly assigned***, in a 1 : 1 ratio, to receive liraglutide (3.0 mg) or volume-matched placebo administered subcutaneously once daily for 56 weeks, followed by 26 weeks of follow-up without treatment. Treatment ***was initiated*** at a dose of 0.6 mg daily for 1 week, and then the dose was increased weekly until the maximum tolerated dose or the 3.0 mg dose (highest dose allowed) ***was reached***. Randomization ***was stratified*** according to pubertal status and glycemic status and was performed with the use of an interactive Web response system, in permuted blocks, with block sizes of 4. Lifestyle therapy continued from the start of the trial to week 82.	To show that the trial began sometime in the past and is complete, *the past tense* is used: *received, fulfilled, were randomly assigned, was initiated, was increased, was reached, was stratified.* However, when it states a fact, the present tense is employed: *is provided.*

- **The Point of View and Voices**

The Original Article	Comment
Trial Oversight ***We conducted*** this randomized, double-blind, placebo-controlled, phase 3 trial from September 29, 2016, through August 8, 2019, at 32 sites in five countries. ***The trial had*** a 12-week run-in period, a 56-week treatment period, and a 26-week follow-up period without treatment. The trial protocol with the statistical analysis plan is available at NEJM.org. ***The trial was designed and overseen*** by representatives of the trial sponsor with input from selected site investigators. ***The site investigators gathered*** the data, and ***the sponsor performed*** the data analyses. ***All the authors had*** full access to the data, ***directed and supervised*** the data analyses, ***interpreted*** the data, and vouch for the accuracy and completeness of the data and the fidelity of the trial to the protocol. ***The first author wrote*** the first draft of the manuscript with assistance from an independent medical writer funded by the sponsor. ***The manuscript was subsequently revised and approved*** by all the authors, who agreed to submit the manuscript for publication.	This Trial Oversight employs both point of the trial results and point of the experimenters. When it stresses the point of the experimenters, the aspect of active voice is generally used: *we conducted, the trial had, the investigators gathered, the sponsor performed...* When it stresses the point of trial results, the aspect of passive voice is used: *the trial was designed, the manuscript was revised and approved.*
Statistical Analysis ***We hypothesized*** that liraglutide would show superiority to placebo with regard to weight reduction in adolescents. For the primary end point of the change from baseline in the BMI standard deviation score at week 56, ***we calculated*** that a sample of 228 participants would provide the trial with 90% power to show a significant treatment effect, with a standard deviation in the liraglutide group of 0.35 and an estimated treatment difference (i.e., difference between the liraglutide group and the placebo group) of −0.26. ***Primary and secondary efficacy end points were analyzed*** according to the intention-to-treat principle, with analyses including all participants who had undergone randomization with imputations for participants who were lost to follow-up.	In the statistical analysis, when it stresses the point of the experimenter (we), the aspect of active voice is generally used: *We hypothesized, we calculated...* The aspect of passive voice is employed to stress the trial results: *Primary and secondary efficacy end points were analyzed...*

- **The Use of Parentheses**

The Original Article	Comment
Participants ...Pubertal adolescents ***(12 to <18 years of age)*** were eligible for inclusion in the trial if they met the following criteria: obesity, defined as a body mass index ***(BMI; the weight in kilograms divided by the square of the height in meters)*** that corresponded to an adult value of 30 or more...	1. Specific or detailed information 2. Clinical definitions or terms

continued

The Original Article	Comment
Trial Procedures and End Points ...Randomization was stratified according to pubertal status (Tanner stage 2 or 3 vs. Tanner stage 4 or 5) and glycemic status ***(normoglycemia vs. prediabetes or type 2 diabetes)*** and was performed with the use of an interactive Web response system, in permuted blocks, with block sizes of 4. Lifestyle therapy continued from the start of the trial to week 82...	Specific or detailed information
Trial Procedures and End Points ...Treatment was initiated at a dose of 0.6 mg daily for 1 week, and then the dose was increased weekly until the maximum tolerated dose or the 3.0mg dose ***(highest dose allowed)*** was reached ***(Fig. S1)***...	1. Additional explanations 2. Appendix and Figures

5. Key Points

- The Materials and Methods section answers the three core questions:
  ① What was used? (The study subjects)
  ② What was done? (The study design and interventions)
  ③ How was it done? (The methods of measurements, calculations and statistical analysis)
- The hypothesis and experimental approach can serve as the topic sentence for the protocol or study design section.
- The study design should have a consistent point of view, either that of the research, or that of the researchers.
- The verbs in past tense are generally used for explaining the steps that were taken.
- The subtitles can signal transitions between subsections. The format of the subsections is changed on the basis of target journals.
- The parentheses are necessary for maintaining the natural flow of ideas.
- The choice of the point of view is decided by the stress on the point of the experiment (the passive voice) or on the point of the experimenter (the active voice) when writing the methods section.

6. Revision Exercise

Direction: The following paragraph from a study design needs revision before being used. Read it, answer the following questions and then revise it.

To determine whether contact with children increases self-awareness among elderly people, the incidence of age related accidents in the home was compared between two groups of elderly men and women. Two hundred elderly men and women were chosen by matching age gender and cognitive function. They were then divided into two groups: group A had contact with children at least one hour per day, 6 days per week; group B had contact with children less than or equal to one hour per week. At the end of 1 year, data from the number of visits to emergency rooms or doctor's offices for treatment of accidents in the home was compared between the two groups. Any accidents related to the presence of children were factored out of the study results. No significant difference was found between the incidence of accidents in the home between the two groups.

1. Which section of a research paper would include this paragraph?
2. Independent Variable (s):
3. Dependent Variable (s):
4. Population:
5. Which sentence should be omitted?
6. Writing mechanics problem:
7. Correct the grammar in the sentence that begins with "At the end of 1 year, ..."
8. Write a topic/phrase title for this paper.

Chapter Ten Results

Key Concepts

Data

Comparison

Results

Clarity

1. The Function of the Results Section

1.1 Function of the results section

The **RESULTS** section answers the question "**what was found in the research?**" As the "heart" of the paper, it presents the most relevant results corresponding to the research question raised in the '**Introduction**' section, gives results about all measurements and outcomes in the '**Methods**' section and provides basis for interpretation of results in the '**Discussion**' section. At this point in the paper, the **hypothesis** has been provided in the '**Introduction**' and the **method** for collecting the support data has been provided in the '**Materials and Methods**' section. Now the relationship between the data collected and the hypothesis must be provided. Here the **Results** section is to take that extra step by translating the raw data into meaningful results with skillful use of text, figures and tables to tell a complete, focused and interesting story.

1.2 Distinction between results and data

The **Results** section includes both results and data presented in text, tables and figures. Distinction needs to be made between results and data (Table 1).

Table 1 Difference between Data and Results

Data	**Results**
Are the facts (often numbers) obtained from experiments or observations.	Are the meaning and interpretation of data
Can be presented as raw (e.g. concentration of a measured variable), summarized (e.g. mean and SD), or transformed (e.g. percentage).	Are expressed as statements that explain or summarize what the data show
Can rarely stand alone	May have a direction (e.g. decrease, increase) or magnitude, e.g. 2-fold, 10% increased
	May contain statistical significance, e.g. *P* value
E.g. mean (SD) fasting blood glucose was 180 (20) mg/dL in patients with type 2 diabetes. Mean fasting blood glucose was 95 (5) mg/dL in non-diabetic subjects.	E.g. mean fasting blood glucose was significantly higher in patients with type 2 diabetes than in non-diabetic subjects [180 (20) vs. 95 (5) mg/dL, $P = 0.010$][a].

[a]The text presented in square brackets is data and the remainder is a result.

Source: doi: 10.5812/ijem.92113.

The **Methods** section provides the raw data; however, alone, raw data are usually not meaningful. In other words, **Results** section analyzes data at a higher level, and highlights relationships, patterns and trends. By providing the results, authors elucidate the data and make them meaningful. Examples 1 and 2 illustrate the differences between data and results.

Example 1

The average time for exiting the maze decreased in the control group by 14 seconds over the 7-day period. The average time for exiting the maze decreased in the experimental group by 19 seconds over the same period.

Example 2

The average time for exiting the maze decreased significantly more in the experimental group than in the control group over the 7-day period (Fig. 2).

Example 1 provides the raw data, but does not provide the meaningful result. Example 2 transforms the raw data into a meaningful result through a comparison of the two groups. Although the readers are not given the raw data, they should be directed to a figure or table that contains the data (Example 2).

In writing, results are presented in the text; data (the most important) in figures and tables, with a limited amount in the text, which are usually included in square brackets following the results. Results without data or data without results should be avoided. The text of the Results section needs to state the main messages derived from a table or figure so that readers do not need to interpret data themselves. Tables are used to present specific information or exact values while figures are used to show comparisons, patterns or trends. Statistically relevant information, such as sample size, *P* values and the types of statistics, are also presented.

2. The Content and Structure of the Results Section

2.1 Content

The primary content of the Results section presents the most relevant findings relating to the central research question raised in the Introduction section, no matter whether they support the hypothesis or not. Secondary findings including results relating to secondary outcomes and sub-group analyses are also given. Results for both experimental and control groups and of each item mentioned in the Materials and Methods should be given. Comparison of the study results with others, and discussion and interpretation of the results are not recommended, for these belong to the Discussion section.

2.2 Structure

In terms of structure, the Results section typically starts with a description of the characteristics of study participants (number, gender, age and symptoms), which indicate the comparability of the study groups at baseline. For clinical trials, the number of patients completing the protocol, and those lost, excluded or withdrawn should also be given. Authors may also comment on whether baseline characteristics are statistically similar or different. Reporting guidelines may differ with different study types and specific journals.

Generally, findings from the primary analyses are given first, followed by secondary findings and subgroup analyses, and additional or unexpected findings. The Results section needs using a combination of text, tables and figures.

The Results section should be organized logically, either in chronological order, from general to specific, from most to least important, or by topic/study groups or experiment/measured parameters. Results in chronological order present results in the same order as methods using subtitles that parallel results. Results organized from general to specific usually proceed from general findings, such as characteristics of overall study population, to more specific findings including data and results for each group. This organization pattern is mostly employed in clinical studies involving multiple groups of individuals receiving different treatments. The third pattern, from most to least important, is employed when authors want to immediately highlight important findings which answer the main question. The last pattern is employed when, for example, diagnostic and analytical performance of a number of assays for analytes is compared.

3. The Writing Principles for the Results Section

The Results section needs to be clear, concise and objective. It is essential to employ all the writing skills to present key findings in an orderly and logical sequence with illustrative materials and text. Clarity, conciseness and objectiveness are the guiding principles for writing this section.

3.1 Clarity

Clarity means the results should be pertinent to the research question, and data should be centered on those essential for readers to understand the findings. Writers do not need to devote equal length to all results, but need to emphasize important results and subordinate secondary information, such as irrelevant and peripheral information. These results would integrate with the whole picture of the paper, echoing the main research aim. In this way, readers would not be confused and distracted with excessive experimental details, and would be presented with a comprehensive and supported argument.

In writing this section, three important strategies could ensure clarity: giving clear comparisons, writing clear topic sentences and managing accurate time representations.

(1) Comparisons

Comparing results is an important part of the Results section, as the result is often expressed through a comparison of two or more measurements. There are several correct structures for making comparisons, and there are several incorrect structures that lead to ambiguous interpretations. Look at the following examples:

Example 3

The average time for exiting the maze decreased 26% more in the experimental group compared with the control group over the 7-day period (Fig. 2).

Example 3 is ambiguous; it could have three different interpretations:

- The experimental group had a greater decrease in time than did the control group.
- The experimental group had a decrease in time, but the control group had no decrease.
- The experimental group took less time than did the control group.

To avoid this ambiguity the word ***than*** should be used rather than ***compared with*** (Example 4). The variable that has changed (the average time for exiting the maze) becomes the subject of a verb (decreased) that expresses the type of change that is being compared between the two groups. The two groups then follow in parallel prepositional phrases on either sides of the ***than***.

Example 4

The average time for exiting the maze decreased *more* in the experimental group *than* in the control group.

For emphasis, either group can be moved to a position directly following the verb (Example 5). However, to preserve a parallel comparison, the pronoun ***that*** should placed directly after the ***than***. One way to ensure a correctly worded comparison is to notice whether the comparison word (more) and the ***than*** are separated or together. If separated, no pronoun (***that***) is necessary (Example 4). If the comparison word and the ***than*** are together in the sentence a pronoun is necessary (Example 5).

Example 5

The average time for exiting the maze decreased in the experimental group 26% *more than* that in the control group.

(2) Topic Sentences

In the Results section, the message of the topic sentences should be a result, not a method. However, a method can be expressed in a transition phrase (Example 6) or as the subject of the topic sentence (Example 7).

Example 6

After consumption of oranges, the maze exit time decreased. (Method as a transition phrase, result in the subject and verb)

Example 7

Consumption of oranges decreased the maze exit time. (Method as subject of the sentence, result in the verb and object)

The goal is to emphasize the important results and not to allow them to become obscure by less important details. This can be done by making sure that the topic sentence expresses an important result, and by ordering the details from most to least important, as can be seen by comparing the following examples.

Example 9 is an improvement over Example 8 because:

- The topic sentence is a result rather than a method.
- The method is used as a transition phrase in the topic sentence to provide the details about both groups and the experiment.
- Details are provided in parentheses and a figure rather than in the main text.
- Results are provided rather than data.

Example 8

The 10 rats, 5 in the experimental group and 5 in the control group, were timed as they solved the maze exit problem over the course of the 3-week experiment. The average times for exiting the maze for the experimental group were 44 seconds at 7 days, 39 seconds at 14 days and 36 seconds at 21 days. The average times for the control group were 42 seconds at 14 days, 40 seconds at 36 days and 40 seconds at 21 days. The times for one of the rats in the experimental group actually increased over the 28 days. After completion of the experiment, it was found that this rat had a cancerous tumor of the liver. If the data from this rat are excluded the average times are reduced to 42, 38, and 34 seconds respectively.

Example 9

After testing both the experimental group (n = 5) and the control group (n = 5) 3 times over the 21-day experiment, we found that the time for solving the maze exit problem decreased significantly more in the experimental group than in the control group ($P < 0.001$) (Fig. 1). In fact, the decrease in the experimental group is even greater if the data from one rat that was later discovered to have liver cancer are excluded.

Example 11 is an improvement over Example 10 because:

- Only results that are relevant to the hypothesis are included.
- The results are arranged from most to least important.

Example 10

The rats were divided into three experimental groups. The first group was fed 10 grams of dried orange per day, the second group was fed 15 grams of dried orange per day and the third group was fed 20 grams of dried orange per day throughout the 21-day experiment. The average time for solving the maze exit problem did not decrease significantly more in group one and two than in the control group, but the average time decreased significantly more in the third group than in the control group ($P < 0.001$). In the third group, the significant decrease took place between the 7th and the 14th day of the experiment, with no further decrease between the 14th day and the 21st.

Example 11

The time for solving the maze exit problem decreased significantly more than that in the control group only in the third experimental group (Fig 2). However, the difference was only significant between the 7th and 14th day, with no significant difference between the 14th and the 21st day.

(3) Tenses

The Results section mainly uses past tense. The past tense is used for reference to results obtained in hypothesis-testing papers. However, the present tense is used for reference to non-textual elements, e.g. *Table 1 shows..., the findings confirm..., the data suggest..., we believe that...*

3.2 Conciseness

Conciseness means writers do not need to include irrelevant and peripheral information, including overview sentences, unnecessary intensifiers and unnecessary nominalizations (Kallestinova, 2011).

Overview sentences only announce the topic instead of giving the message; a suggestion for revising overview sentences is to integrate the message in the sentence. Example 13 is an improvement of Example 12 as it replaces the overview expressions with the message.

Example 12

To show our results, we first introduce all components of experimental system and then describe the outcome of infections.

Example 13

Components of experimental systems are..., and infections led to...

Wordiness in the Results section can be avoided by carefully checking the use of unnecessary intensifiers such as "*clearly*", *"essential", "quite", "basically", "rather", "fairly", "really" and "virtually"*, as they actually lower the credibility of the results rather than intensify them. So avoid using the above-mentioned terms in describing figures and tables.

Another strategy for reducing wordiness is checking unnecessary nominalizations. These nominalizations are nouns derived from verbs or adjectives, and are used with weak verbs like *"be", "have", "do", "make", "cause", "provide" and "get"*. A possible solution is to replace the weak verbs with verbs embedded in the nominalization.

Example 15 is an improvement of Example 14 as it replaces the overview expressions with the message. Example 17 is an improvement of Example 16. Examples 15 &17 highlight the key information and make it clear to the readers by the verb instead of hiding them in the vague and abstract nominalizations.

Example 14

...we tested the hypothesis that there is a disruption of membrane asymmetry...

Example 15

...the membrane asymmetry is disrupted...

Example 16

...in this paper, we provide an argument that stem cells repopulate injured organs...

Example 17

...In this paper, we argue that...

3.3 Objectiveness

Objectiveness is key to the Results section and constitutes a core component of academic ethics. Writers are suggested to exclude irrelevant results but not to ignore valid anomalous results that contradict the research hypothesis or do not support the current scientific literature. Data manipulation or falsification, in texts or in figures and tables, is a willful distortion of data and results and violates research ethics. Contradictory results should not be avoided; they need to be mentioned, if possible, explained.

4. Case analysis

4.1 Case 1

Case 1 is from the article titled "Associations between push-up exercise and future cardiovascular events among active adult men" (doi: 10.1001/jamanetworkopen.2018.8341), which reports a retrospective longitudinal cohort study. This paper aims to evaluate the association between push-up capacity and subsequent cardiovascular disease (CVD) event incidence in a cohort of active adult men. The Results section falls into two subsections 'Study population' and 'Association of push-ups and CVD-related outcomes'.

JAMA Network | Open

Original Investigation | Nutrition, Obesity, and Exercise

Association Between Push-up Exercise Capacity and Future Cardiovascular Events Among Active Adult Men

Justin Yang, MD, MPH; Costas A. Christophi, PhD; Andrea Farioli, MD, PhD; Dorothee M. Baur, MD, MS; Steven Moffatt, MD; Terrell W. Zollinger, DrPH; Stefanos N. Kales, MD, MPH

A. The General Structure Analysis

The Structure of Results

Subsections	Description	Comment
Subsection 1	Study Population	In terms of structure, this section is organized from general to specific. The only paragraph describes descriptive characteristics of participants included in the cohort. It follows the principle of conciseness by only reporting important baseline characteristics in Table 1 (here age and BMI), and summarizing and interpreting the data in the table, pointing out associations between push-up capacity and risk factors for CVD in the text while including data in brackets rather than listing these data in the text.
Subsection 2	Association of Push-ups and CVD-Related Outcomes	There are **3 paragraphs**, describing the association of push-ups and CVD-related outcomes, comparing first the relationship between the two, then results of Cox regression models for association of push-ups and VO_2 max groups with CVD outcomes, and lastly Kaplan-Meier curves for the cumulative risk of CVD outcome events. The topics of these three paragraphs correspond to the three types of statistical analyses in the Method section. The main message in each paragraph is invariably introduced at the first or second sentence of each paragraph. **Para. 1** describes Table 2. **Para. 2** describes Table 3. **Para. 3** describes the Figure.

B. The Language Features

- **The Tenses Used**

The Results section mostly employs two kinds of tenses, the present tense and the past tense.

Tables and figures are mainly referred as "***Table/Figure... shows***" in the present tense, while other verbs are in the past tense.

The Tenses Used

The Original Article	Comment
Study Population A total of 1562 eligible firefighters ***underwent*** baseline examination between February 2, 2000, and November 12, 2007, and ***were included*** in the initial retrospective cohort. Mean (SD) age at baseline for all participants ***was*** 39.6 (9.2) years and the mean (SD) BMI was 28.7 (4.3). ***Table 1 shows*** the baseline characteristics of the 1104 participants for whom push-up information was available stratified by push-up capacity at baseline examination. As summarized in Table 1, push-up capacity ***was found*** to be significantly inversely associated with most of the baseline risk factor variables that we examined (age, $P < .001$; BMI, $P < .001$; systolic blood pressure, $P < .001$; diastolic blood pressure, $P < .001$; total cholesterol level, $P = .02$; low-density lipoprotein cholesterol level, $P = .04$; triglycerides, $P < .001$; glucose level, $P < .001$; and smoking status, $P < .001$), although it was significantly positively associated with the estimated VO_2 max ($P < .001$). The baseline characteristics of firefighters without push-up data ***were*** similar and not statistically different from those who completed the push-up capacity evaluation on all markers of CVD risk.	To show the final results, *the past tense* is used: *underwent, were included, was, was found* ... To state the tables and figures, *the present tense* is used: *Table 1 shows...*
Association of Push-ups and CVD-Related Outcomes During the 10-year follow-up period, 37 CVD-related outcomes (1104 participants, 8601 person-years) ***occurred*** among firefighters with recorded push-up capacity data at baseline and were included in our analyses (Table 2). ***We observed*** significantly lower CVD IRRs in all groups with higher push-up capacity compared with the group with the lowest baseline push-up capacity. Participants able to complete more than 40 push-ups ***had*** a 96% reduction in incident CVD events compared with those completing fewer than 10 push-ups (IRR, 0.04; 95% CI, 0.01-0.36). In comparison, ***we observed*** similar crude IRRs of CVD outcomes when stratifying the cohort by estimated VO_2 max baseline. ***Table 3 shows*** the results of the Cox regression models for the association of push-ups and VO_2 max groups with CVD outcomes. Even after adjusting for age and BMI, ***we observed*** an independent association of push-up capacity with CVD outcomes. Increased capacity ***was associated*** with a lower risk for CVD outcomes, with the comparison of the 21- to 30-push-up group vs. the 0- to 10-push-up group being statistically significant (hazard ratio, 0.25; 95% CI 0.08-0.76), although the other group comparisons did not reach statistical significance. ***The Figure shows*** Kaplan-Meier curves for the cumulative risk of CVD outcome events for each category of baseline push-up capacities, with the 0- to 10-push-ups group having the greatest cumulative incidence of CVD outcome events. ***The Figure shows*** a 15% cumulative incidence of CVD events in the 0 to 10 push-ups group vs. 5% or lower in the other groups.	To show the final results, *the past tense* is used: *occurred, observed, had* ... To state the tables and figures, *the present tense* is used: *Table 3 shows...*

- **The Point of View and Voices**

The Original Article	Comment
Study Population A total of 1562 eligible firefighters ***underwent*** baseline examination between February 2, 2000, and November 12, 2007, and ***were included*** in the initial retrospective cohort. Mean (SD) age at baseline for all participants ***was*** 39.6 (9.2) years and the mean (SD) BMI was 28.7 (4.3). ***Table 1 shows*** the baseline characteristics of the 1104 participants for whom push-up information was available stratified by push-up capacity at baseline examination. As summarized in Table 1, push-up capacity ***was found*** to be significantly inversely associated with most of the baseline risk factor variables that we examined (age, $P < .001$; BMI, $P < .001$; systolic blood pressure, $P < .001$; diastolic blood pressure, $P < .001$; total cholesterol level, $P = .02$; low-density lipoprotein cholesterol level, $P = .04$; triglycerides, $P < .001$; glucose level, $P < .001$; and smoking status, $P < .001$), although it was significantly positively associated with the estimated VO_2 max ($P < .001$). The baseline characteristics of firefighters without push-up data ***were*** similar and not statistically different from those who completed the push-up capacity evaluation on all markers of CVD risk.	The Results section mostly employs both the point of the results and point of the experimenter (we), study population, or the tables and figures. When it stresses the point of the results, the aspect of passive voice is generally used: *was included, was found...* The use of the passive voice thus makes the results prominent in the sentence. It also can help achieve objectivity and high consistency within this subsection or paragraph. When it stresses the point of the study population or tables, figures, the aspect of active voice is generally used: *Firefighters underwent, Table 1 shows...*
Association of Push-ups and CVD-Related Outcomes During the 10-year follow-up period, 37 CVD-related outcomes (1104 participants, 8601 person-years) occurred among firefighters with recorded push-up capacity data at baseline and were included in our analyses (Table 2). ***We observed*** significantly lower CVD IRRs in all groups with higher push-up capacity compared with the group with the lowest baseline push-up capacity. Participants able to complete more than 40 push-ups ***had*** a 96% reduction in incident CVD events compared with those completing fewer than 10 push-ups (IRR, 0.04; 95% CI, 0.01-0.36). In comparison, ***we observed*** similar crude IRRs of CVD outcomes when stratifying the cohort by estimated VO_2 max baseline. ***Table 3 shows*** the results of the Cox regression models for the association of push-ups and VO_2 max groups with CVD outcomes. Even after adjusting for age and BMI, ***we observed*** an independent association of push-up capacity with CVD outcomes. Increased capacity ***was associated*** with a lower risk for CVD outcomes, with the comparison of the 21- to 30-push-up group vs. the 0- to 10-push-up group being statistically significant (hazard ratio, 0.25; 95% CI 0.08-0.76), although the other group comparisons did not reach statistical significance. ***The Figure shows*** Kaplan-Meier curves for the cumulative risk of CVD outcome events for each category of baseline push-up capacities, with the 0- to 10-push-ups group having the greatest cumulative incidence of CVD outcome events. ***The Figure shows*** a 15% cumulative incidence of CVD events in the 0- to 10-push-ups group vs. 5% or lower in the other groups.	When it stresses the point of the experimenter (we), the aspect of active voice is generally used: *We observed... Table 3 shows... The Figure shows...*

- **The Comparison**

The Original Article	Comment
Table 2 We observed ***significantly lower*** CVD IRRs in all groups with higher push-up capacity ***compared with*** the group with the lowest baseline push-up capacity. Participants able to complete more than 40 push-ups had a ***96%*** reduction in incident CVD events compared with ***those*** completing fewer than 10 push-ups.	Comparisons are described skillfully in this paper. How comparison is described is a tough job. A good strategy is to choose the noun phrase, especially the subject of the clause. Actually, clarity and conciseness can be achieved by integrating the message, that is, the specific change or trend (*lower, reduction, increased...*) with the variable we are comparing. The first sentence begins with a signal phrase "**we observed**" to introduce a key finding of the study, that CVD IRRs was found to be "significantly lower" in "all groups with higher push-up capacity" than in "the group with the lowest baseline push-up capacity". The object of the simple sentence "**significantly lower CVD IRRs**" is carefully chosen and makes the comparison clear and concise. Instead of using a complex sentence "*we observed that CVD IRRs was significantly lower in all groups... compared with the group with the lowest...*", the writers use the simple "subject + verb+ object" sentence pattern, which is "*we observed+ comparative adjective + variable in Group A compared with Group B*". The comparative phrase "*compared with*" links the two groups. In addition, the group with the lowest capacity is subordinated to the latter part of the sentence to set up the baseline for comparison.
Association of Push-ups and CVD-Related Outcomes ...***Participants*** able to complete more than 40 push-ups had a ***96% reduction*** in incident CVD events compared with ***those*** completing fewer than 10 push-ups (IRR, 0.04; 95% CI, 0.01-0.36). In comparison, ***we observed*** similar crude IRRs of CVD outcomes when stratifying the cohort by estimated VO_2 max baseline.	This sentence begins with "participants", so the writer is comparing participants in the two groups, rather than comparing the two groups. The object "96% reduction in incident CVD events" also integrates the message "*96% reduction*" with the topic "*incident CVD events*", and enables the comparison to be described with a simple sentence pattern "*participants in Group 1... had a percentage + change+ compared with those in Group 2*". The pronoun "*those*" is used in the latter half of the sentence to refer to participants in order to avoid repetition, and "*96% reduction*" quantifies the difference. Careful readers may have found that the above sentences for comparison all used the phrase "*compared with*".

4.2 Case 2

Case 2 is the article titled "A Randomized Trial of E-Cigarettes versus Nicotine-Replacement Therapy" published on *The New England Journal of Medicine* (doi: 10.1056/NEJMoa1808779).

The NEW ENGLAND JOURNAL *of* MEDICINE

ORIGINAL ARTICLE

A Randomized Trial of E-Cigarettes versus Nicotine-Replacement Therapy

Peter Hajek, Ph.D., Anna Phillips-Waller, B.Sc., Dunja Przulj, Ph.D., Francesca Pesola, Ph.D., Katie Myers Smith, D.Psych., Natalie Bisal, M.Sc., Jinshuo Li, M.Phil., Steve Parrott, M.Sc., Peter Sasieni, Ph.D., Lynne Dawkins, Ph.D., Louise Ross, Maciej Goniewicz, Ph.D., Pharm.D., Qi Wu, M.Sc., and Hayden J. McRobbie, Ph.D.

This paper is to evaluate the 1-year efficacy of refillable e-cigarettes as compared with nicotine replacement when provided to adults seeking help to quit smoking and combined with face-to-face behavioral support. This Results section has four subsections: Participants, Effects of treatment on abstinence, Treatment adherence and ratings and Effects on withdrawal symptoms and safety evaluation.

A. The General Structure Analysis

The Structure of Results

Subsections	Description	Comment
Subsection 1	Study Population	Structurally, this section follows the order from general to specific. All paragraphs in this section use results as topic sentences. **Para. 1** describes the participants information. As a clinical trial, the number of clients undergoing randomization and those completing the follow up are reported. Detailed participants baseline characteristics were referred to Table 1 and Table S1. Not all information was listed in the tables; only two key features ("these smokers are middle-aged and 40.7% entitled to free prescriptions") were summarized.

continued

Subsections	Description	Comment
Subsection 2	Effects of Treatment on Abstinence	**Subsections 2~4** are organized in the order of importance, starting with the primary outcome to secondary outcomes. **Subsection 2** includes 3 paragraphs and presents the effects of treatment on abstinence. **Para. 1** starts with the primary outcome—the higher rate of sustained 1-year abstinence in the e-cigarette group than in the nicotine-replacement group. **Para. 2** describes the results of a post-hoc analysis. **Para. 3** describes secondary outcomes concerning abstinence and relapse rates.
Subsection 3	Treatment Adherence and Ratings and Effects on Withdrawal Symptoms	Subsection 3 includes **4 paragraphs** organized exactly in the order of outcomes announced in the subheading. **Para. 1~2** report the results of overall adherence and among participants with 1-year abstinence. **Para. 3** describes the satisfaction ratings for e-cigarettes and nicotine-replacement products. **Para. 4** reports the effects of treatment on withdrawal symptoms.
Subsection 4	Safety Evaluation	Subsection 4 comprises **4 paragraphs:** participants' death, serious adverse events, adverse reactions and respiratory symptoms. These are actually in the order announced in the 'measures' section of METHOD.

B. The Language Features

- **The Tenses Used**

This Results section is basically written in the past tense with tables and figures referred to in brackets except only one sentence. This is different from the last case, so journals do differ in their ways of presenting data, and authors need to consult the author guidelines in each journal for specifics.

The Tenses Used

The Original Article	Comment
Treatment Adherence and Ratings and Effects on Withdrawal Symptoms Overall adherence ***was*** similar in the two groups, but e-cigarettes ***were used*** more frequently and for longer than nicotine replacement ***(Table 3)***. In the nicotine-replacement group, 88.1% of participants ***used*** nicotine-replacement combinations. In the e-cigarette group, practically all participants ***used*** refillable e-cigarettes ***(Table S4 in the Supplementary Appendix)***.	To show the final results, *the past tense* is used: *was, were used, provided, reported...*

continued

The Original Article	Comment
Among participants with 1-year abstinence, 80% (63 of 79) ***were*** using e-cigarettes at 52 weeks in the e-cigarette group and 9% (4 of 44) ***were*** using nicotine replacement in the nicotine-replacement group. Further details of product use (including the use of nonassigned products) ***are*** provided in the Supplementary Appendix, including Tables S4 and S5. Both e-cigarettes and nicotine-replacement products ***were*** perceived to be less satisfying than cigarettes. However, e-cigarettes ***provided*** greater satisfaction and ***were*** rated as more helpful to refrain from smoking than nicotine replacement products (*Table S6 in the Supplementary Appendix*). Among participants with abstinence at 1 week after their quit date as well as participants with abstinence at 4 weeks, those in the e-cigarette group ***had*** less severe urges to smoke than did those in the nicotine-replacement group (*Table 4*). They also ***reported*** a smaller increase from baseline in irritability, restlessness, and inability to concentrate than those in the nicotine-replacement group during the first week of abstinence. Between-group differences in hunger and depression ***were*** in the same direction but less substantial. By week 4, participants in either group who ***were*** abstinent ***reported*** little withdrawal discomfort (*Table S7 in the Supplementary Appendix*).	Tables and figures were mostly referred to in brackets. Except in the last sentence in Para. 2 in this subsection. "*Further details of product use (including the use of nonassigned products)* **are** *provided in the Supplementary Appendix, including Tables S4 and S5.*" Although the sentence does not begin with a table or figure as the subject, it is describing information in tables, so the present tense is used.

- **The Point of View and Voices**

The Original Article (part)	Comment
Participants A total of 2045 clients of stop-smoking services ***were screened***, and 886 ***underwent*** randomization (439 to the e-cigarette group and 447 to the nicotine-replacement group). Of the randomly assigned participants, 78.8% ***completed*** the 52-week follow-up (Fig. 1). The sample ***was composed*** largely ***of*** middle-aged smokers, with 40.7% entitled to free prescriptions (a marker of social disadvantage or poor health) (Table 1, and Table S1 in the Supplementary Appendix).	The Results section mostly employs both the point of view of the results, the experimenter (we) and study population. Both active and passive voices are used. In this subsection, both active and passive voices are used to describe the study population. The change of voice helps maintain consistency of topic in this paragraph. *886 underwent...78.8% completed...* *were screened, was composed of...*

continued

The Original Article (part)	Comment
Effects of Treatment on Abstinence The rate of sustained 1-year abstinence ***was*** 18.0% in the e-cigarette group and 9.9% in the nicotine-replacement group (relative risk, 1.83; 95% confidence interval [CI], 1.30 to 2.58; $P < 0.001$) (Table 2). The absolute difference in the 1-year abstinence rate between the two groups ***was*** 8.1 percentage points, resulting in a number needed to treat for one additional person to have sustained abstinence of 12 (95% CI, 8 to 27). The result ***did not change*** substantially in the four sensitivity analyses (relative risk, 1.75 to 1.85; $P \leqslant 0.001$ for all comparisons) (Table S2 in the Supplementary Appendix). Abstinence rates ***were*** higher in the e-cigarette group than in the nicotine-replacement group at all time points (Table 2, and Table S3 in the Supplementary Appendix). We ***conducted*** a post hoc analysis, in which participants with 1-year abstinence who used nonassigned products (see the Supplementary Appendix) ***were removed*** from the sample (3% [2 of 79] in the e-cigarette group were using nicotine replacement and 20% [9 of 44] in the nicotine-replacement group were using e-cigarettes). This ***resulted*** in a 1-year abstinence rate of 17.7% in the e-cigarette group, as compared with 8.0% in the nicotine-replacement group (relative risk, 2.21; 95% CI, 1.52 to 3.22). Among participants in whom full abstinence ***was*** not ***achieved***, more ***had*** a carbon monoxide–validated reduction of smoking by at least 50% in the e-cigarette group than in the nicotine replacement group (Table 2). Time to relapse and relapse rates at 52 weeks among participants with sustained abstinence at 4 weeks ***did not differ*** substantially between the two trial groups (hazard ratio for time to relapse, 1.14; 95% CI, 0.96 to 1.34; relative risk of relapse at 52 weeks, 1.27; 95% CI, 0.93 to 1.73).	When it stresses the point of view of the results, the aspect of active voice is generally used: *was, did not change, did not differ...* When it stresses the point of view of the experimenter (we), the aspect of active voice is also used: *We conducted...* In certain sentences, passive voice is also used: *were removed, was not achieved.* The use of the passive voice in these cases serves to highlight the relevant results.
Treatment Adherence and Ratings and Effects on Withdrawal Symptoms Overall adherence ***was*** similar in the two groups, but e-cigarettes ***were used*** more frequently and for longer than nicotine replacement (Table 3). In the nicotine-replacement group, 88.1% of participants ***used*** nicotine-replacement combinations. In the e-cigarette group, practically all participants ***used*** refillable e-cigarettes (Table S4 in the Supplementary Appendix). Among participants with 1-year abstinence, 80% (63 of 79) ***were using*** e-cigarettes at 52 weeks in the e-cigarette group and 9% (4 of 44) ***were using*** nicotine replacement in the nicotine-replacement group. Further details of product use (including the use of nonassigned products) ***are*** provided in the Supplementary Appendix, including Tables S4 and S5. Both e-cigarettes and nicotine-replacement products ***were perceived*** to be less satisfying than cigarettes. However, e-cigarettes ***provided*** greater satisfaction and ***were rated*** as more helpful to refrain from smoking than nicotine replacement products (Table S6 in the Supplementary Appendix). ...	When it stresses the point of view of the results or study participants, the aspect of active voice is generally used: *used, were, were using, provided, ...* When it stresses the point of view and the results, passive voice can also be used: *are provided, were perceived...* The change of voice helps maintain consistency in this subsection.

continued

The Original Article (part)	Comment
Safety Evaluation Two participants ***died*** during the trial. One ***died*** from ischemic heart disease in the e-cigarette group and one from traumatic spine injury in the nicotine-replacement group. There ***were*** 27 serious adverse events in the e-cigarette group and 22 in the nicotine-replacement group (Table S8 in the Supplementary Appendix). No serious adverse event in either group ***was classified*** by the trial clinician as being related to product use, but ***we noted*** 1 respiratory event in the nicotine-replacement group and 5 in the e-cigarette group. Of the prespecified adverse reactions of interest, nausea ***was reported*** more frequently in the nicotine-replacement group and throat or mouth irritation more frequently in the e-cigarette group. There ***was*** little difference between the two groups in the percentage of participants reporting severe nausea or severe throat or mouth irritation. Regarding the prespecified respiratory symptoms of interest, the incidence of cough and phlegm production ***declined*** in both trial groups from baseline to 52 weeks. However, among participants who reported cough or phlegm at baseline, significantly more ***were*** symptom-free at the 52-week follow-up in the e-cigarette group than in the nicotine-replacement group. To determine whether this was due to the higher abstinence rate in the e-cigarette group, ***we ran*** an exploratory analysis that controlled for abstinence status at 52 weeks. This did not change the results.	When it stresses the point of the study population or results, the aspect of active voice is generally used: *died, were...* Passive voice is also used for certain results to achieve consistency: *was classified..., was reported...* When it stresses the point of view of the experimenter (we) , the aspect of active voice is also used: *We noted, we ran...*

- **The Comparison**

The Original Article	Comment
Effects of Treatment on Abstinence "The rate of sustained 1-year abstinence was ***18.0% in the e-cigarette group** and **9.9% in the nicotine-replacement*** group (relative risk, 1.83; 95% CI, 1.30 to 2.58; $P < 0.001$) (Table 2)"...	In terms of language features, a typical feature is how outcomes are compared in clinical trials between different groups with the help of parallel structures, and how ideas are linked logically with transition words. Parallel structures describe similar ideas in similar forms, and thus facilitate understanding. We can put both phrases and sentences in parallel position. By putting two noun phrases describing abstinence rates, *18.0% in the e-cigarette group* and *9.9% in the nicotine-replacement group* in parallel position, repetition is avoided without reducing the information load of the sentence.

continued

The Original Article	Comment
Treatment Adherence and Ratings and Effects on Withdrawal Symptoms Overall adherence was similar in the two groups, ***but*** e-cigarettes were used ***more frequently*** and ***for longer than*** nicotine replacement (Table 3)... Among participants with 1-year abstinence, 80% (63 of 79) were using e-cigarettes at 52 weeks in the e-cigarette group ***and*** 9% (4 of 44) were using nicotine replacement in the nicotine-replacement group.	Besides noun phrases, comparative adverbs can also be put in a parallel structure. The "*but*" clause describes two features of e-cigarettes; that is, it is used "*more frequently*" and "*for longer*". Instead of using two separate sentences to describe the comparison, the authors put the adverb phrase "*more frequently*" in parallel with "*for longer than*", and thus achieved conciseness. Moreover, sentences can also be put in parallel structures. Similar sentence structures can be found in the clauses before and after the conjunction "*and*". Parallel structures are useful tools for expressing similar concepts, actions and messages. Try to use them when you are reporting results, especially in clinical trials, where outcomes in both the experimental and the group receiving standard treatments or the control group need to be reported.
"***Both*** e-cigarettes and nicotine-replacement products were perceived to be less satisfying than cigarettes. ***However***, e-cigarettes provided greater satisfaction and were rated as more helpful to refrain from smoking than nicotine-replacement products (Table S6 in the Supplementary Appendix)."	Another language feature is the use of *transition words*, which describe logical relationships in a sentence and a paragraph. This paragraph begins with similarities between the two products, as signaled by "*both*"; more details concerning the difference between the two is signaled by "*however*".
"Among participants with abstinence at 1 week after their quit date as well as participants with abstinence at 4 weeks, those in the e-cigarette group had less severe urges to smoke than did those in the nicotine-replacement group (Table 4). They ***also*** reported a smaller increase from base-line in irritability, restlessness, and inability to concentrate than those in the nicotine-replacement group during the first week of abstinence. Between-group differences in hunger and depression ***were in the same direction but less substantial***. By week 4, participants in either group who were abstinent reported little withdrawal discomfort (Table S7 in the Supplementary Appendix)."	This paragraph begins with difference in "urge to smoke" between the two products, and "*also*" in the second sentence provides one more aspect of difference. The third sentence uses "*were in the same direction but less substantial*" to link the third aspect of difference by pointing out both the nature and the degree of comparison. The skillful use of words signaling similarity (*both, also*), difference (*however, but*) and degree (*less substantial*) ensures the description of various outcomes in a clinical trial to flow naturally from one to the other, without causing boredom and tiredness.

5. Key Points

- The function of the Results section is to translate data into meaningful results. It presents the most relevant results corresponding to the research question raised in the Introduction and highlights the important results; subordinate control results, methods and data. Translate data into meaningful results.
- The Results section is arranged from the most to the least important and from the primary outcomes to the secondary outcomes.
- The message of the topic sentences in this section should be a result, not a method.
- The results and data should be reported in an objective, accurate and consistent manner.
- Text, tables and figures are effective in stating the results. It is not necessary to restate similar results in both textual and non-textual elements (figures and tables).
- Language resources including comparative structures, transition words and parallel structures help to achieve clarity and conciseness.

6. Revision Exercise

Direction: The following paragraph from a Results section needs revision before being used. Read it, answer the following questions and then revise it.

Nearsightedness was tested for a correlation with time spent reading a cellphone in 200 teenagers. Over the course of the 4-year study, nearsightedness increased significantly more in teenagers that spent 20 or more hours per week reading a cell phone compared with teenagers that spent less than 5 hours per week reading a cell phone, no significant difference was found between students that spent no time reading a cellphone and those that read a cellphone from 5 to 10 hours per week. Figure 2 shows the data for all groups tested.

1. Which section of a research paper would include this paragraph?
2. Independent Variable (s):
3. Dependent Variable (s):
4. Revise the topic sentence:

5. Revise the faulty comparison in the 2nd sentence:
6. Writing mechanics error:
7. Write a message, sentence title for this paper:
8. Point out one change you would make to the last sentence:

Chapter Eleven Discussion

Key Concepts

Application	Implication
Recommendation	Speculation

1. The Function of the Discussion Section

The **DISCUSSION** section is the last part of the IMRaD formatted research paper, if there is not a separate Conclusion section. With the question raised in the Introduction, materials and methods described in the Materials and Methods, and data and results reported in the Results, it is now the moment to give a clear answer to the question.

The function of the **Discussion** section is to clearly show the answer, and to prove that the answer or explanation or description provided by the study is now the best possible. This section should thus provide both empirical and logical evidence to show this and should provide links between the answer, explanation or description and the applicable fields of study to show the importance of what has been uncovered.

Simply, the **Discussion** section shows what has been uncovered is true and important. It acts as the global positioning system (GPS) to show how far the authors have moved with this study on the science road. A well-polished discussion could convince readers of both the validity and importance of the "bit of truth" that has been found, and thus leave readers a strong final impression.

2. The Content and Structure of the Discussion Section

2.1 Content

Since the main function of the Discussion section is to show that what has been uncovered is true and important, this section should begin with a clear expression of the findings.

(1) What is the Answer?

In a hypothesis-testing paper, the Discussion section should begin with a sentence that contains the answer to the question or hypothesis posed in the Introduction. This sentence serves as a topic sentence that provides the message of the entire Discussion section. The sentence should match the hypothesis sentence used at the end of the Introduction (Example 1) in that it should use the same key terms for the variables and population, and the same verb, but the sentence will have a new signal phrase or clause (Example 2) to clearly show the function of the sentence. In Example 2, the verb in the signal clause is in the past tense (*determined*) to reflect the completed action; however, the verb in the answer, *increases*, remains in the present tense as it is in the hypothesis.

Example 1

This study was designed to test the hypothesis that eating oranges increases intelligence in rats.

Example 2

This study determined that eating oranges increases intelligence in rats.

The Discussion section can begin with the topic sentence that contains the answer, or it can begin with a restatement of the question followed by the answer, if this delay would help the readers to understand. However, the answer should come as early as possible. The more that is included before the answer, the less powerful the answer will be, so it is usually counter-productive to include another introduction or a restatement of the results before providing the answer. After the answer has been provided, a transition phrase or clause (Example 3) should be used to introduce the Discussion section's first subtopic, which is usually the empirical evidence or results that support the answer.

Example 3

- The evidence is that...
- Our experiments found that...
- In our experiments...

(2) Why is the Answer True? (Empirical and Logical Support)

At this point, the results from both the present study and from other studies are presented to provide both empirical and logical support for the answer. The results are usually best organized from the most to the least important with separate paragraphs and topic sentences for each important result.

After the supporting results have been provided, any necessary explanation of the logical relationship between the results and the answer should be provided. This will include defense against contradictions between the present study and other studies, as well as an explanation of any results from the present study that do not support the answer. Each instance of defense or explanation should be placed in a separate paragraph that begins with a topic sentence that provides either the topic or the topic and message of the paragraph.

Before transitioning from the support to the importance of the answer, any extra pieces that do not seem to fit into the categories of results, explanation or defense can be inserted. This could include explanations for any assumptions or contradictions within the study design, or any surprising findings that do not necessarily relate to the answer. These extras should also be well organized in separate paragraphs, each with its own topic sentence. At this point, if the Discussion section has been organized well, it should now be possible to follow the logical progression of the section by reading only the first sentence from every paragraph.

(3) Why is the Answer Important? (Connecting the Answer to Related Fields)

The Discussion section moves from the answer to the support, which is often organized from the most to the least important. Thus, it is unavoidable that the strong impression from the beginning will weaken. At this point it would be very ineffective to make a vague statement about how further research is needed followed by a conclusion that restates the answer. A better way to come to a close would be to show the importance of the paper by connecting the answer to the related fields. This can be done by showing the practical or theoretical impact of the new discovery. By ending with a practical or theoretical use, the reader is left with a lasting impression of the importance of the study.

(4) What is the Practical Use? (Applications and Recommendations)

Applications and recommendations are nearly the same; they are both practical immediate uses that the answer has provided. However, they differ in that an application implies stronger support than does a recommendation. The difference is made clear through a signal phrase as well as the verb choice.

Applications imply the strongest support. Because of this, the statement of an application requires no softening through signal phrases or modal verbs (Example 4), or sometimes can be softened with modal verbs indicating greater possibility such as *can* or *will*. Recommendations are marked as a recommendation by the main verb and often softened with the modal verb *should* (Example 5).

Example 4

The conclusions reported here provide a safe and effective method for increasing cognitive performance.

Example 5

Based on the conclusions reported here, we *recommend* that citrus fruits *should* be considered as an essential addition to all school lunch programs.

(5) What is the Theoretical Use? (Implications and Speculations)

Implications and speculations are not as well supported as applications and recommendations, so they may or may not have an immediate practical use. However, they are important for providing direction for further research. An implication is the next logical step in an argument. Although it has no empirical support as of yet, it does have logical support. An implication is signaled with the verb *suggest* or *imply* and is softened with the modal verb *may* or *might* (Example 6). A speculation does not even require much logical support. It is a guess based on what is already known. Speculations are signaled with the verb *speculate* and softened with the modal verb *may* or *might* (Example 7).

Example 6

The conclusions reported here *suggest* that cognitive function *may* be partially dependent on the consumption of specific nutrients.

Example 7

The conclusions reported here cause us to *speculate* that improving the diet of primary school students from impoverished areas *might* help to reduce the learning gap between the rural and urban areas.

By providing connections between the answer and the related fields, the paper can now come to a powerful close. Although it is probably always true that further research is necessary, it is much more effective to give a direction for the further research through an implication or speculation than to merely state the obvious, that further research is needed.

Different signal phrases and verb choices for application, recommendation, implication or speculation are presented in the following table to show the difference between the four types (Table 1).

Table 1 Signal Phrases and Verbs

Types	Main Verb	Modal Verb
Application	—	can, will
Recommendation	recommend	should
Implication	suggest, imply	may, might
Speculation	speculate	may, might

2.2 Structure

The Discussion section follows the cone structure, zooming out from main findings to the research context, including statement of the answer, explanation of the answer, and presentation of strengths and limitations and importance of the study.

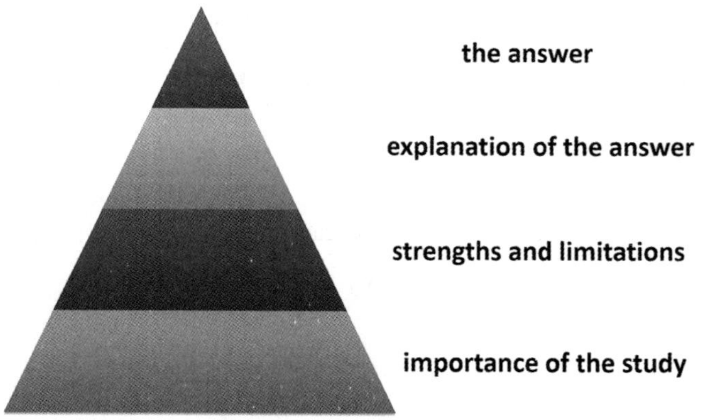

(1) Stating the Answer

Starting the discussion is challenging. A better choice can be to start with the study's major findings that provide an answer to the research question in the Introduction. It is better to answer the question exactly as it was asked, using the same key terms for variables and population, the same verb where appropriate, and the same point of view (specify the population/animal). Sometimes it is better to remind the readers of the research question, even provide a brief context, and then state the answer.

(2) Supporting and Explaining the Answer

After the answer has been introduced, it is time to show how the study contributes to existing knowledge in the field of interest, and how the findings fit into the general picture of the current research. Support of the answer includes results from both the present study and other studies. In a clearly written discussion, these results are organized from the most to the least important.

Relationship between the results and the answer should be explained after support for results is given. Explanations include theoretical or empirical justifications for validity of the results; discrepancies between the present study and others, discrepancy between pieces of results in the study, and unexpected results might distort the general picture of the study, so explanations and defenses need to be given. Explanations describe why the answer is reasonable and how it fits in with the literature.

(3) Pointing out Strengths and Limitations

Next, strengths and limitations of the study are analyzed. Strengths could be related to the study objectives, participants or methods. Be careful to claim priority with absolute statements including "*for the first time*" or "*wholly explains*". If the need to claim priority is strong, the claim could be softened with words like "*to our knowledge, this is the first study...*".

No study is perfect. It is important to outline the scope of the study by pointing out limitations and weaknesses, and clarify assumptions of the study. It is wise to focus on the limitation that matters, rather than beat around the bush by listing general weaknesses that also fit other studies. Only listing the problems might not be a good idea, as these problems might override the findings. Do not forget to explain why the limitations, weaknesses, and assumptions are acceptable. In other words, try to provide feasible explanations or solutions.

(4) Establishing Importance

If the target journal does not require a separate conclusion section, then it is necessary to add a paragraph with the "take-home message" — the main conclusion based on the study findings. The paper could end with the importance of the study described as an application, recommendation, implication or speculation, or with a final paragraph, which restates the answer. Either way, readers could be left with a final impression of the importance of the study. Making broad claims, strong statements and vague conclusions like "*more work is needed to be done*" should be avoided. Another tip is to avoid overstating the importance of the study. Do not over-inflate the generalizability of the findings and avoid claim importance for results that fail to reach statistical significance.

3. The Writing Principles of the Discussion Section

It is important to keep the Discussion section results-driven; that is, only findings reported in the Results section should be discussed. Writers are not suggested to present findings that have not been described in the Methods or Results section, or to discuss what they had hoped to find but did not.

Present the answer to the research question or hypothesis with the same variables, verbs used and point of view with those in the question from the introduction section. The answer needs to be given in the first or one of the first sentences of the Discussion Section. Commonly used chunk phrases for giving answers are:

- *This study shows that...*
- *Our results suggest/indicate/findings demonstrate that...*
- *In this study, we provide evidence that...*
- *In this study, we have shown that...*
- *In this study, we have found that...*
- *In this study, we found that...*

Provide references for key arguments. Commonly used chunk phrases for supporting and explaining the answer are:

- *...lend credence to...*
- *...provide support for...*
- *We found that...*

- *The evidence is that...*
- *Evidence that (state the answer) is that...*
- *(State the answer) has been demonstrated in the following way...*
- *... is also reminiscent of.../consistent with our findings/our findings are in keeping with...*
- *As confirmed in/in contrast with previous/other researches...*
- *In contrast/compared with the literature...*
- *a finding that conflicts with the answer to the question;*
- *... this finding cannot be attributed to...rather, it appears...*

Limitations should be specific to the study. Commonly used chunk phrases for pointing out limitations are:

- *Another limitation of our method...*
- *The imprecision...could have arisen from limitations of the method...*
- *Despite these limitations, our method has advantages over those previously used...*
- *This is a reasonable assumption because...*

End the discussion section by connecting the answer to the world through an application, recommendation, implication or speculation. Commonly used chunk phrases for describing importance are:

- *...should be reconsidered...*
- *...need to be...*
- *...are crucial for/is essential to...*

Use the active voice and first person pronouns. Writing of the Discussion section should convey confidence and authority. One effective way is to use the active voice and first person pronouns.

4. Case Analysis

4.1 Case 1

Case 1 is an article titled "Living near major roads and the incidence of dementia, Parkinson's disease, and multiple sclerosis: a population-based cohort study" published on *The Lancet* (doi.org/10.1016/ S0140-6736 (16)32399-6).

Articles

Living near major roads and the incidence of dementia, Parkinson's disease, and multiple sclerosis: a population-based cohort study

Hong Chen, Jeffrey C Kwong, Ray Copes, Karen Tu, Paul J Villeneuve, Aaron van Donkelaar, Perry Hystad, Randall V Martin, Brian J Murray, Barry Jessiman, Andrew S Wilton, Alexander Kopp, Richard T Burnett

The research question raised in the Introduction section is "we sought to investigate the association between exposure to traffic, measured by residential proximity to major roadways, and the incidence of dementia, Parkinson's disease, and multiple sclerosis in a large population-based cohort in Ontario, Canada".

A. The General Structure Analysis

The Structure of Discussion

Subsections	Description	Comment
Subsection 1	Stating the answer	Structurally, this article follows the cone shape structure of the discussion section, starting from stating the answer of the study, to supporting and explaining the answer with other studies, and finally to the broader research context by describing the limitations and research importance. **Subsection 1** is the 1 paragraph and presents the answer to the question. It corresponds closely to the question raised in the INTRODUCTION.

continued

Subsections	Description	Comment
Subsection 2	Supporting and explaining the answer	**Subsections 2** includes 3 paragraphs. It supports and explains the answer by connecting the study to other research. **Para. 1** first states the novelty of the study, describing it as the first one to investigate the onset of three major neurodegenerative diseases in association with near-roadway exposure. It then describes other studies investigating the association between living near major roads and brain health, and thus supports the findings of the present study. It also explains the possible mechanisms for the association, listing possible mechanisms like systemic inflammation. **Para. 2** moves on to explain an important finding of the study—why $PM_{2.5}$ and NO_2 cannot fully explain the near-road effect on dementia, pointing to noise as a potential factor. **Para. 3** further supports and explains another finding of the study—the association between traffic exposure and Parkinson's disease and multiple sclerosis. It does so by examining other studies investigating the issue, and explaining why no association was found in the present study.
Subsection 3	Pointing out limitations and strengths	**Subsections 3** includes 4 paragraphs. It points out the limitations and strengths of the present study. **Para. 1** describes the inability to identify undiagnosed cases of dementia, Parkinson's disease, and multiple sclerosis through the current study design. **Para. 2** describes the lack of information on medications that might potentially influence dementia risk. **Para. 3** describes the lack of accuracy concerning personal exposure to air pollution and noise. **Para. 4** describes the 3 strengths of the study: large population, quantifying and comparing the effects on three major neurodegenerative diseases and the availability of detailed information on medical and residential history.
Subsection 4	Establishing importance	The last paragraph is the conclusion. It restates the answer of the study, and points to a theoretical implication.

B. The Language Features

- **The Tenses Used**

This Discussion section is written in past, present and present perfect tenses. When methods or results of already completed studies (including the present study) are referred to, past tense is used. Present perfect tense is used for describing a series of related research findings, and also in some cases for results of a specific study. Present tense is used for describing accepted research facts, explaining and interpreting findings and evaluating the present study.

The Tenses Used

The Original Article	Comment
In this large population-based cohort, living near major roadways ***was associated with*** increased dementia incidence. The associations ***seemed*** stronger among urban residents, especially those living in major urban centres and those who never moved. Although the increase in risk might appear moderate (eg, HRs varied from 1.07–1.12 for living <50 m away from a major road, depending on the region), ***this translates to*** 7–11% of dementia cases in patients who live near major roads attributable to traffic exposure (appendix). The associations ***were*** robust to various sensitivity analyses, except for additional adjustment for $PM_{2.5}$ and NO_2 which led to a modest attenuation. It ***is*** noteworthy that both NO_2 and $PM_{2.5}$ ***were*** positively associated with dementia. Lastly, ***we found*** no association between roadway proximity and incidence of Parkinson's disease or multiple sclerosis.	To describe specific findings of the present study, *the past tense* is used: *was associated with, seemed, were, we found...* To interpret the findings and evaluate the present study, *the present tense* is used: *this translates to..., It is noteworthy that..., this is the first study to...*
To our knowledge, ***this is the first study to*** investigate the onset of three major neurodegenerative diseases in association with near-roadway exposure. Previous studies ***have linked*** living near roadways to cognitive decline in cohorts of older adults in Boston MA, USA and in the Ruhr area, Germany, and to smaller white matter hyperintensity volume in the Framingham Off spring cohort. Living near major roads substantially ***increases*** an individual's exposure to traffic-related air pollution (eg, ultrafine particles, nitrogen oxides, and particles from wear of tyres and friction materials), and noise. Although the mechanisms through which traffic exposure might affect brain health ***are*** unknown, systemic inflammation arising from traffic-related air pollution ***is*** probably important. In studies of both experimental animals and in autopsy samples of sudden accidental deaths in human beings, particulates and diesel exhaust ***provoke*** oxidative stress and systemic inflammatory responses, disrupt the blood-brain barrier, precipitate Aβ peptides, and activate microglia. Ultrafine particles ***have*** also ***been found*** in the olfactory bulb and the frontal cortical areas in the brain of highly exposed dogs and human beings. Furthermore, emerging epidemiologic evidence ***relates*** nitrogen oxides and black carbon, markers for traffic-related pollution, to dementia incidence and cognitive impairment...	To describe a series of related research findings, *the present perfect tense* is used: *have linked* To describe accepted research facts, *the present tense* is used: *increases, is, relates* To describe a specific research finding, *the present perfect tense* is used: *have been found, has been linked to*
The fact that $PM_{2.5}$ and NO_2 ***did*** not fully explain the near-road effect on dementia ***suggests*** that additional pollutants or other factors such as noise might play a role. Although we ***were unable to*** directly examine these factors, traffic-related noise ***has been linked*** to cognitive impairment in a cohort in Germany. In rat models, noise exposure directly ***impaired*** cognition...	To describe specific findings of already completed studies, *the past tense* is used: *did, were unable to, impaired...* To interpret the findings, *the present tense* is used: *suggests*

continued

The Original Article	Comment
Our study ***has*** some limitations. First, we could not identify undiagnosed cases of dementia, Parkinson's disease, and multiple sclerosis. However, the estimates ***were*** unchanged when we ***adjusted*** for access to neurologists, a North/South indicator, deprivation, and time trends. With universal health care in Ontario, incomplete diagnosis might lead to underestimation of the true effect because this measurement error ***was*** probably independent of the exposure.	To evaluate the study, *the present tense* is used: *has* To describe specific methods and findings of the present study, *the past tense* is used: *adjusted, was, lacked, controlled...*
Second, we ***did*** not have information on medications that might potentially influence dementia risk (eg, antiinflammatory medication and NSAIDs), although it ***is*** unclear whether these factors would be associated with traffic exposure. Furthermore, we ***lacked*** information on individual socioeconomic status and behavioural variables. To control for these unmeasured variables, we ***adjusted for*** neighbourhood socioeconomic status and comorbidities. Since neighbourhood socioeconomic status ***is*** strongly associated with individual socioeconomic status and behavioural variables, and comorbidities and neurodegenerative diseases ***share*** some common behavioural factors, adjusting for these variables should reduce the influence of these unmeasured variables on HR (appendix). We further ***controlled*** indirectly for these variables, and ***found*** similar results. Although we cannot rule out residual confounding, the null findings for Parkinson's disease and multiple sclerosis ***do*** not support this possibility.	To describe accepted research facts, *the present tense* is used: *is, share*
Conclusions In this large cohort, living near major roadways ***was*** associated with higher incidence of dementia, but not Parkinson's disease or multiple sclerosis. Given the potentially significant implications of traffic exposure on dementia risk, understanding the effect of different aspects of traffic ***merits*** further investigation.	To describe findings of the present study, *the past tense* is used: *was* To interpret findings of the study, *the present tense* is used: *merits*

- **The point of view and voices**

The Original Article	Comment
In this large population-based cohort, living near major roadways ***was associated with*** increased dementia incidence. The associations ***seemed*** stronger among urban residents, especially those living in major urban centres and those who never moved. Although the increase in risk might appear moderate (eg, HRs varied from 1.07–1.12 for living <50 m away from a major road, depending on the region), ***this translates to*** 7–11% of dementia cases in patients who live near major roads	The Discussion section employs the point of view of the results, the experimenter (we) and other experimenters (previous studies). Both active and passive voices are used. In the 1st Para., both active and passive voices are used to describe the answer.

continued

The Original Article	Comment
attributable to traffic exposure (appendix). The associations ***were*** robust to various sensitivity analyses, except for additional adjustment for $PM_{2.5}$ and NO_2 which led to a modest attenuation. It ***is*** noteworthy that both NO_2 and $PM_{2.5}$ ***were*** positively associated with dementia. Lastly, ***we found*** no association between roadway proximity and incidence of Parkinson's disease or multiple sclerosis.	When it stresses the point of view of the results, the aspect of active voice is generally used: *seemed, translates to, were...* In certain sentences, passive voice is also used: *was associated with...* The use of the passive voice in these cases helps maintain consistency of topic in this paragraph. When it stresses the point of view of the experimenter (we) , the aspect of active voice is also used: *We found...*
To our knowledge, ***this is*** *the first study to* investigate the onset of three major neurodegenerative diseases in association with near-roadway exposure. ***Previous studies have linked*** living near roadways to cognitive decline in cohorts of older adults in Boston MA, USA and in the Ruhr area, Germany, and to smaller white matter hyperintensity volume in the Framingham Off spring cohort. Living near major roads substantially ***increases*** an individual's exposure to traffic-related air pollution (eg, ultrafine particles, nitrogen oxides, and particles from wear of tyres and friction materials), and noise. Although the mechanisms through which traffic exposure might affect brain health ***are unknown***, systemic inflammation arising from traffic-related air pollution ***is*** probably important. In studies of both experimental animals and in autopsy samples of sudden accidental deaths in human beings, particulates and diesel exhaust ***provoke*** oxidative stress and systemic inflammatory responses, disrupt the blood-brain barrier, precipitate Aβ peptides, and activate microglia. Ultrafine particles ***have*** also ***been found*** in the olfactory bulb and the frontal cortical areas in the brain of highly exposed dogs and human beings. Furthermore, emerging epidemiologic evidence ***relates*** nitrogen oxides and black carbon, markers for traffic-related pollution, to dementia incidence and cognitive impairment. ***We observed*** that exposures to NO_2 and $PM_{2.5}$ ***were related to*** dementia and that adjusting for these two pollutants attenuated its association with roadway proximity, suggesting that the effect of traffic exposure might, at least in part, operate through this mechanism. Given the potentially significant implications of exposure to traffic related pollutants on dementia risk, understanding their effects ***merit*** further investigation.	The active voice helps convey confidence and authority of the authors. In this paragraph supporting and explaining the answer, both active and passive voices are used. When it stresses the point of view of the results, the aspect of active voice is used: *this is..., increases, merits...* Passive voice is also used when the point of view of the results is stressed: *...are unknown, have been found...* The use of the passive voice in these cases helps maintain consistency of topic in this paragraph. When it stresses the point of view of other experimenters, the aspect of active voice is also used: *Previous studies have linked...* When it stresses the point of view of the experimenter (we) , the aspect of active voice is also used: *We observed...*

continued

The Original Article	Comment
Our study ***has*** some limitations. ... Second, we ***did*** not have information on medications that might potentially influence dementia risk (eg, antiinflammatory medication and NSAIDs), although it ***is*** unclear whether these factors would be associated with traffic exposure. Furthermore, we ***lacked*** information on individual socioeconomic status and behavioural variables. To control for these unmeasured variables, we ***adjusted for*** neighbourhood socioeconomic status and comorbidities. Since neighbourhood socioeconomic status ***is*** strongly ***associated with*** individual socioeconomic status and behavioural variables, and comorbidities and neurodegenerative diseases ***share*** some common behavioural factors, adjusting for these variables should reduce the influence of these unmeasured variables on HR (appendix). We further ***controlled*** indirectly for these variables, and ***found*** similar results. Although we cannot rule out residual confounding, the null findings for Parkinson's disease and multiple sclerosis ***do not support*** this possibility.	Both active and passive voices are used in describing strengths and limitations. When it stresses the point of view of the experimenter (we) , the aspect of active voice is also used: *We did not, we lacked information, we adjusted for...* The use of active voice explains the efforts taken by the experimenters to make up for the limitations, and thus increases validity of the study. When it stresses the point of view of the results, the aspect of active voice is used: *share, do not support* Passive voice is also used occasionally: *is associated with.*
Conclusions In this large cohort, living near major roadways ***was associated with*** higher incidence of dementia, but not Parkinson's disease or multiple sclerosis. Given the potentially significant implications of traffic exposure on dementia risk, understanding the effect of different aspects of traffic ***merits*** further investigation.	When the conclusion stresses the point of view of the results, both active and passive voices are used: *was associated with, merits further investigation.* The change of voice maintains the consistency of the topic of the paragraph.

- **Presenting the answer and limitations**

The Original Article	Comment
In this large population-based cohort, living near major roadways ***was associated with*** increased dementia incidence...Lastly, ***we found*** no association between roadway proximity and incidence of Parkinson's disease or multiple sclerosis.	This case illustrates well how the answer to the question in the discussion corresponds to the question in the Introduction. The answer should be presented with the same variables and verbs with those in the question from the introduction section. In this example, the answer lies in the first sentence of the Discussion section. In this study, the predictor variable is "exposure to traffic", which is measured by "residential proximity to major railways", and the outcome variable is the incidence of dementia, Parkinson's disease and multiple sclerosis.

continued

The Original Article	Comment
	The experimental design is also specified in the research question as "a large population-based cohort". The answer begins with a description of the research design, which used exactly the same words as those in the research question "the large population based cohort". The authors slightly paraphrased description of the predictor variable in the answer and they used "living near major roads" and "roadway proximity". The outcome variable in the answer used the same key words as those in the question, which is "the incidence of dementia" and "incidence of Parkinson's disease or multiple sclerosis". The verbs "was associated with" and "found no association" echo the word "association" in the research question. So in this example, basically the authors used the same key words and the same verbs in the answer with those in the question.
Our study has some limitations. First, we could not identify undiagnosed cases of dementia, Parkinson's disease, and multiple sclerosis. ***However, the estimates were unchanged*** when we adjusted for access to neurologists, a North/South indicator, deprivation, and time trends. With universal health care in Ontario, incomplete diagnosis ***might lead to underestimation*** of the true effect because this measurement error was probably independent of the exposure. ***Second***, we did not have information on medications that might potentially influence dementia risk (eg, antiinflammatory medication and NSAIDs), although it is unclear whether these factors would be associated with traffic exposure. Furthermore, we lacked information on individual socioeconomic status and behavioural variables. ***To control for these unmeasured variables***, we adjusted for neighbourhood socioeconomic status and comorbidities. Since neighbourhood socioeconomic status is strongly associated with individual socioeconomic status and behavioural variables, and comorbidities and neurodegenerative diseases share some common	Limitations are also well described. The authors point out four limitations in the study. The first sentence serves as the topic sentence for this subsection. The four limitations are signaled clearly by the phrases "first" "second", "third", and "finally". All the limitations discussed are specific to this particular study instead of general weaknesses that might apply to all studies. The first limitation describes the problem in identifying undiagnosed cases of the three neurodegenerative diseases. But the author immediately clarifies the effort they have taken for reducing the influence of the problem and assures the readers that "the estimates were unchanged" and points out the possible implication of the problem. The word 'might' shows the prudence of the writers. The second limitation concerns the lack of information on medications that might potentially influence dementia risk, and on individual socioeconomic status and behavioural variables. Again, the author establishes validity of their study by reporting what has been done to control for the unmeasured variables, reasons for making these efforts, results of these further analyses and possible implications.

continued

The Original Article	Comment
behavioural factors, ***adjusting for these variables should reduce*** the influence of these unmeasured variables on HR (appendix). ***We further controlled indirectly for these variables, and found similar results***. Although we cannot rule out residual confounding, the null findings for Parkinson's disease and multiple sclerosis do not support this possibility. ***Third... Finally...***	So when possible, after presenting the limitations, authors can try to provide explanations and justifications for these limitations. This can not only improve the validity of the study, but also display the prudence and care of the authors.

4.2 Case 2

Case 2 is an article titled "Association of Migraine With Aura and Other Risk Factors With Incident Cardiovascular Disease in Women" published on *JAMA* (doi: 10.1001/jama.2020.7172).

Research

JAMA | Original Investigation

Association of Migraine With Aura and Other Risk Factors With Incident Cardiovascular Disease in Women

Tobias Kurth, MD, ScD; Pamela M. Rist, ScD; Paul M Ridker, MD, MPH; Gregory Kotler, PhD; Vadim Bubes, PhD; Julie E. Buring, ScD

The aim was to compare the adjusted incidence rate of CVD between women with migraine with aura, women with migraine without aura or no migraine, and women with other major vascular risk factors.

A. The General Structure Analysis

The Structure of Discussion

Subsections	Description	Comment
Subsection 1	Stating the answer	Structurally, this article follows the cone shape structure of the discussion section, starting from stating the answer of the study, to supporting and explaining the answer with other studies, and finally to the broader research context by describing the limitations and research importance. **Subsection 1** is the 1 paragraph and states the answer to the question. It echoes the research purpose raised in the INTRODUCTION.
Subsection 2	Supporting and explaining the answer Pointing out strengths	**Subsections 2** includes 3 paragraphs. It supports and explains the answer by connecting the study to other research. **Para. 1** compares the present study with other studies investigating the association of migraine and migraine with aura on overall and specific CVD events. It also points out the novelty of the present study at the end of this paragraph. **Para. 2** moves on provide several biological mechanisms that could explain the link between migraine and increased risk of CVD events. **Para. 3** describes the strengths of the present study.
Subsection 3	Pointing out limitations	**Subsections 3** includes 1 paragraph pointing out the limitations of the present study. In this *JAMA* article, strengths of the study are included in the second subsection, while statements of limitations are put in a separate subsection. So journals may vary in their presentation of different components of the discussion section, and readers are suggested to consult author guidelines before submitting their research.
Subsection 4	Establishing importance	The last paragraph is the conclusion. It restates the answer of the study, and points to a theoretical implication.

- **The Tenses Used**

This Discussion section in this case is also written in past, present and present perfect tenses. When methods or results of already completed studies (including the present study) are referred to, past tense is used. Present perfect tense is used for describing a series of related research findings, and also for evaluating the current research status. Present tense is used for describing accepted research facts, explaining and interpreting findings and evaluating the present study.

The Original Article	Comment
In this large cohort study of women aged at least 45 years, women with migraine with aura ***had*** a higher incidence rate of self-reported major CVD events compared with women without migraine or with migraine without aura, after adjusting for other major vascular risk factors and confounding. Although diabetes and current smoking ***were*** associated with higher rates of major CVD, migraine with aura ***was*** more strongly associated with the rate of major CVD than obesity or unfavorable lipid levels, and ***had*** a similar association as with elevated systolic blood pressure or high total cholesterol. The associatfion patterns ***were*** similar for specific CVD events.	To describe findings of the present study, *the past tense* is used: *had, were, was...*
The association of migraine and migraine with aura on overall and specific CVD events ***has been evaluated*** using relative risk in many clinic- and population-based studies. Although there ***was*** an indication of some heterogeneity across studies, the relative risk estimates ***ranged*** from 1.5 for migraine overall to more than 2 for migraine with aura. In a 2018 nationwide population-based study from Denmark, Adelborg and colleagues ***estimated*** the relative hazard of CVD according to migraine status. Migraine with aura ***was associated with*** myocardial infarction (hazard ratio, 1.74 [95% CI, 1.44-2.11]), ischemic stroke (hazard ratio, 2.49 [95% CI, 2.16- 2.86]), and hemorrhagic stroke (hazard ratio, 1.82 [95% CI, 1.34-2.48]). In contrast to data from the Women's Health Study,[18]migraine without aura ***was*** also ***associated with*** an increased risk of CVD in the study by Adelborg and colleagues,[4] but the effect size ***was*** smaller compared with migraine with aura. A previous study using Women's Health Study data ***observed*** similar incidence rates of major CVD for migraine with aura as seen in this study after adjustment for age. However, to the best of our knowledge, ***no studies have compared*** the estimated adjusted incidence rates of CVD by migraine status with the adjusted incidence rates of CVD due to other cardiovascular risk markers.	To describe a series of related research findings, *the present perfect tense* is used: *has been evaluated...* To describe specific methods or findings of already completed studies, *the past tense* is used: *was, ranged, estimated, was associated with, observed,* To evaluate the current research status, *the present perfect tense* is used: *No studies have compared...* *...have been proposed...* *...have included...*
Several biological mechanisms ***have been proposed*** to link migraine, particularly migraine with aura, with increased risk of CVD events. These mechanisms ***have included*** elevated vascular biomarkers leading to endothelial dysfunction, other vascular pathology, open patent foramen ovale, genetic predisposition, or migraine-specific or other pain medication use. However, with regard to medication use, not only patients with migraine with aura ***use*** such treatment. Cortical spreading depolarization, the electrophysical mechanisms involved inmigraine aura, can play a role in stroke and potentially in other vascular events. Nevertheless, the precise mechanisms linking migraine with aura to CVD incidence ***are*** still not well understood.	To describe accepted research facts, *the present tense* is used: *use, are*
Strengths of this study ***include*** the large number of participants and outcome events, available information on various vascular risk factors, confirmation of CVD events by medical record review, and the homogeneity of the study population, which reduced potential biases, including differences in health care access.	To evaluate the study, *the present tense* is used: *include, has, is*

continued

The Original Article	Comment
Limitations This study ***has*** several limitations. First, information on migraine and vascular risk factors ***were*** self-reported, and misclassification ***is*** possible. Second, migraine with aura and vascular risk factors ***were*** assessed at baseline, and changes in these risk factors over time ***were*** not taken into account. Third, detailed information on management of migraine or vascular risk factors, which may influence CVD risk, ***was*** not available. Fourth, this study ***was conducted*** in a cohort of female health professionals and these results may not be generalizable to other settings, particularly to men. Fifth, this study ***did*** not explore how changes in migraine frequency over time may modify the association between migraine with aura and CVD incidence. Additionally, no information on when migraine started for the participating women ***was*** available.	To describe specific methods and findings of the present study, *the past tense* is used: *were, was conducted, did* To interpret findings of the study, *the present tense* is used: *include, has, is*
Conclusions In this study of female health professionals aged at least 45 years, women with migraine with aura ***had*** a higher adjusted incidence rate of CVD compared with women with migraine without aura or no migraine. The clinical importance of these findings, and whether they generalize beyond this study population, ***require*** further research.	To describe findings of the present study, *the past tense* is used: *had* To interpret findings of the study, *the present tense* is used: *require*

- **The point of view and voices**

The Original Article	Comment
In this large cohort study of women aged at least 45 years, women with migraine with aura ***had a higher incidence rate*** of self-reported major CVD events compared with women without migraine or with migraine without aura, after adjusting for other major vascular risk factors and confounding. Although diabetes and current smoking ***were associated with*** higher rates of major CVD, migraine with aura ***was*** more strongly ***associated with*** the rate of major CVD than obesity or unfavorable lipid levels, and ***had a similar association*** as with elevated systolic blood pressure or high total cholesterol. The association patterns ***were similar*** for specific CVD events.	The Discussion section employs the point of view of the results, other experimenters (previous studies) and the study population. Both active and passive voices are used. In the 1st Para., both active and passive voices are used to describe the answer. When it stresses the point of view of the study population, the aspect of active voice is used: *had a higher incidence rate of...* When it stresses the point of view of the results, the aspect of active voice is used: *had a similar association, were similar.* Passive voice is also used to describe association: *was associated with...* The use of the passive voice helps maintain consistency of topic in this paragraph.

continued

The Original Article	Comment
The association of migraine and migraine with aura on overall and specific CVD events ***has been evaluated*** using relative risk in many clinic- and population-based studies. Although there ***was*** an indication of some heterogeneity across studies, the relative risk estimates ***ranged*** from 1.5 for migraine overall to more than 2 for migraine with aura. In a 2018 nationwide population-based study from Denmark, Adelborg and colleagues ***estimated*** the relative hazard of CVD according to migraine status. Migraine with aura ***was associated with*** myocardial infarction (hazard ratio, 1.74 [95% CI, 1.44-2.11]), ischemic stroke (hazard ratio, 2.49 [95% CI, 2.16- 2.86]), and hemorrhagic stroke (hazard ratio, 1.82 [95% CI, 1.34-2.48]). In contrast to data from the Women's Health Study, migraine without aura ***was*** also ***associated with*** an increased risk of CVD in the study by Adelborg and colleagues, but the effect size ***was*** smaller compared with migraine with aura. A previous study using Women's Health Study data ***observed*** similar incidence rates of major CVD for migraine with aura as seen in this study after adjustment for age. However, to the best of our knowledge, ***no studies have compared*** the estimated adjusted incidence rates of CVD by migraine status with the adjusted incidence rates of CVD due to other cardiovascular risk markers.	Both active and passive voices are used in supporting the answer. When it stresses the point of view of the results, the aspect of active voice is used: *was, ranged...* Passive voice is also used: *has been evaluated, was associated with...* The use of the passive voice helps maintain consistency of topic in this paragraph. When it stresses the point of view of other experimenters, the aspect of active voice is also used: *Adelborg and colleagues[4] estimated..., a previous study observed, no studies have compared...*
Several biological mechanisms ***have been proposed*** to link migraine, particularly migraine with aura, with increased risk of CVD events. These mechanisms ***have included*** elevated vascular biomarkers leading to endothelial dysfunction, other vascular pathology, open patent foramen ovale, genetic predisposition, or migraine-specific or other pain medication use. However, with regard to medication use, not only patients with migraine with aura ***use*** such treatment. Cortical spreading depolarization, the electrophysical mechanisms involved inmigraine aura, can ***play a role*** in stroke and potentially in other vascular events. Nevertheless, the precise mechanisms linking migraine with aura to CVD incidence ***are*** still not well understood.	Both active and passive voices are used in explaining the answer. When it stresses the point of view of the results, the aspect of active voice is used: *have included..., play a role..., are* Passive voice is also used: *have been proposed...* The use of the passive voice helps maintain consistency of topic in this paragraph. When it stresses the point of view of the study population, the aspect of active voice is used: *use.*

continued

The Original Article	Comment
Strengths of this study ***include*** the large number of participants and outcome events, available information on various vascular risk factors, confirmation of CVD events by medical record review, and the homogeneity of the study population, which reduced potential biases, including differences in health care access.	Both active and passive voices are used in describing strengths and limitations. When it stresses the point of view of the results, the aspect of active voice is used: *include, has, is, did not explore...*
Limitations This study ***has*** several limitations. First, information on migraine and vascular risk factors ***were self-reported***, and misclassification ***is*** possible. Second, migraine with aura and vascular risk factors ***were assessed*** at baseline, and changes in these risk factors over time ***were*** not ***taken into account***. Third, detailed information on management of migraine or vascular risk factors, which may influence CVD risk, was not available. Fourth, this study ***was conducted*** in a cohort of female health professionals and these results may not be generalizable to other settings, particularly to men. Fifth, this study ***did*** not ***explore*** how changes in migraine frequency over time may modify the association between migraine with aura and CVD incidence. Additionally, no information on when migraine started for the participating women ***was*** available.	Passive voice is also used to maintain consistency of the topic: *were self reported, were assessed, was conducted*
Conclusions In this study of female health professionals aged at least 45 years, women with migraine with aura ***had*** a higher adjusted incidence rate of CVD compared with women with migraine without aura or no migraine. The clinical importance of these findings, and whether they generalize beyond this study population, ***require*** further research.	The conclusion stresses the point of view of the results, so active voice is used: *had a higher incidence rate, require.*

- **Supporting the answer and concluding the study**

The Original Article	Comment
The association of migraine and migraine with aura on overall and specific CVD events ***has been evaluated*** using relative risk ***in many clinic- and population-***	This case is a good example showing how the present study is supported with other research.

continued

The Original Article	Comment
based studies. Although there was an indication of some heterogeneity across studies, ***the relative risk estimates ranged*** from 1.5 for migraine overall to more than 2 for migraine with aura. In a 2018 nationwide population-based study from Denmark, Adelborg and colleagues estimated the relative hazard of CVD according to migraine status. Migraine with aura ***was associated with*** myocardial infarction (hazard ratio, 1.74 [95% CI, 1.44-2.11]), ischemic stroke (hazard ratio, 2.49 [95% CI, 2.16-2.86]), and hemorrhagic stroke (hazard ratio, 1.82 [95% CI, 1.34-2.48]). ***In contrast to*** data from the Women's Health Study, migraine without aura ***was also associated with*** an increased risk of CVD in the study by Adelborg and colleagues, ***but the effect size was*** smaller compared with migraine with aura. A previous study using Women's Health Study data ***observed similar incidence rates*** of major CVD for migraine with aura as seen in this study after adjustment for age. ***However, to the best of our knowledge, no studies have compared the estimated adjusted incidence rates of CVD by migraine status with the adjusted incidence rates of CVD due to other cardiovascular risk markers.***	In this study, the authors found that women with migraine with aura had a higher incidence rate of self-reported major CVD events compared with women without migraine or with migraine without aura and presented the answer in the first paragraph of the discussion. In this paragraph they come to provide support for their key findings with findings of other studies. As can be seen from the italicized words in this paragraph, the authors described in the topic sentence at the beginning of this paragraph that the association between migraine and CVD events has been evaluated in many studies, and these studies reached a similar relative risk estimate. And then a specific study from Denmark was cited to provide support for the association between the two variables. The authors also included studies that reported inconsistent findings as indicated by "in contrast to", and they explained those findings. In this way, both support and explanation of results are provided. It is noteworthy that the authors did not stop at summarizing related literature, but highlighted the novelty of the present research in the last sentence of the paragraph as signaled by "however" and "to the best our knowledge, no studies…".
Conclusions ***In this study*** of female health professionals aged at least 45 years, women with migraine with aura had a higher adjusted incidence rate of CVD compared with women with migraine without aura or no migraine. ***The clinical importance*** of these findings, and ***whether they generalize beyond this study population***, require further research.	The conclusion of the study is clearly written. It is composed of a restatement of the answer and description of importance of the study, specifically implications of the findings. The answer is women with migraine with aura had a higher adjusted incidence rate of CVD compared with women with migraine without aura or no migraine. It echoes the first sentence in the Discussion, and also the last sentence of the Introduction. Implications of the answer, including clinical importance and implications of the study population is presented. The article thus ends with a very clear take home message.

5. Key Points

- The answer to the research question or hypothesis should be the first or one of the first sentences of the discussion section.
- The answer should match the question from the introduction section including the variables, verb used and point of view.
- The discussion section should end by connecting the answer to the world through an application, recommendation, implication or speculation.

6. Revision Exercise

Direction: Read the following paragraph from a discussion section and revise it.

In this study, we provide evidence that cell phone use was associated with brain tumor. In our ten-year study we found that the incidence of brain tumor was significantly higher in 3, 000 cell phone users than in the national average (Figure 1). In addition, the incidence of brain tumor was positively correlated to the amount of time spent speaking on a cell phone. Although we used statistical instruments to factor out the possibility that a third and unknown variable was the mechanism behind the association, we cannot conclude that cell phone use is the cause of brain tumor. Further research is needed to provide this link.

1. Which section of a research paper would include this paragraph?
2. Independent variable (s):
3. Dependent variable (s):
4. Population:
5. Revise the sentence that contains the research answer:
6. Writing mechanics problem:
7. Write a topic/phrase title for this research:
8. Revise the faulty conclusion:

Chapter Twelve Abstract

Key Concepts

Concise

Coherent

Continuous

Concurrent

1. The Function of the Abstract

The function of the **ABSTRACT** is to prepare readers for the research paper, by providing specific key elements from each of the other sections of the paper. Its secondary function is to provide a stripped down, but complete version of the research paper for readers that only have access to the abstract.

2. The Structure of the Abstract Section

2.1 Formatted as Paragraph

2.1.1 The Structure

The structure of the **Abstract** is the same as the overall structure of the paper: hypothesis, methods, results and answer. The goal is to take the essential messages from the research paper and then to combine them into one clearly written paragraph. The paragraph must be complete within itself for readers who do not have access to the full paper; so no citations or references to figures or tables should be included.

If a background sentence is necessary for understanding the hypothesis, the abstract can start with this sentence. Otherwise, the abstract should start with a restatement of the hypothesis sentence from the Introduction, including the signal phrase, variables and population.

A signal phrase should be used to transition from the hypothesis sentence to the methods. Either the experimental approach from the introduction or a summarized version of the study design can be used. The methods should be used as a transition from the hypothesis to the results that answer the question. Following the results, a signal phrase should be used to present the answer. If a significant part of the research value comes from an application, recommendation, implication or speculation, then it should be included after the answer. It is important to distinguish between any of these and the answer with appropriate signals and modal verbs.

2.1.2 The Features

(1) Being concise

Concise writing can be thought of as the clear expression of a message with as few words as possible. This is especially important for writing an abstract, because of the strict word count constraints from journals. The concept of a concise style is actually a complex relationship between many factors. By taking a look at some of these factors individually, it is possible to come to a better understanding of what a concise writing style actually looks like.

- **No Elaboration**

The message should be expressed clearly one time without repetition.

- **No Excess**

Every word, phrase, clause and sentence should have a clear function. First, make certain that every word serves a purpose within a phrase. By reducing a wordy phrase to its core meaning, wasted words can be eliminated (Example 1). If an adverbial phrase or clause is not a signal phrase for an important subtopic, the entire phrase or clause can often be eliminated (Example 2).

Example 1

At some *point in time* the mixture will become solid.

At some *time* the mixture will become solid.

Example 2

It is well known that these molecules are unstable.

These molecules are unstable.

(2) Being coherent

Coherence is a relationship between at least two factors: logical flow and continuous flow of ideas. Logical flow of ideas can be achieved by using a topic sentence and sequencing the details that follow according to the function of the paragraph. In the **Abstract**, this logical flow follows the same order as the paper itself: hypothesis, methods, results and then answer. The continuous flow of ideas can be achieved by eliminating gaps in the logical argument and by connecting each idea to the next with signal and transition phrases.

(3) Being concurrent

Concurrence is an effective way to express maximum meaning in minimum space. By changing related clauses into phrases they can be expressed concurrently (at the same time) in a single clause (Example 3).

Example 3

Three rats were included in the control group and were isolated for 4 days.

The *three control rats* were isolated for 4 days.

2.2 Structured with Subheadings

To save time for practitioners structured abstracts are often used. A structured abstract breaks away from the traditional format and briefly provides the important points of the study by subheadings. Journals differ widely on the format for abstracts so it is essential to carefully follow the specific journal's guidelines for writers. Example 4 illustrates possible subheadings for a structured abstract. In Example 4 *Objective* and *Conclusion* correspond to the research question and answer.

Example 4

- Objective
- Methods
- Results
- Conclusion

The advantage of a **Structured Abstract** is that readers can quickly find the element of the research that is relevant to their particular situation or interest. A structured abstract will be even more concise than an abstract formatted as a paragraph. If it is possible to provide the information under the subheadings with a noun phrase rather than a complete sentence, this is acceptable and possibly even preferential.

3. Case Analysis for Structured Formatted Abstract

3.1 Case 1

Case 1 is a structured abstract from the article titled "Anticholinergic Drug Exposure and the Risk of Dementia: A Nested Case-Control Study" published on *JAMA International Medicine* (doi: 10.1001/jamainternmed.2019.0677).

Research

JAMA Internal Medicine | Original Investigation

Anticholinergic Drug Exposure and the Risk of Dementia
A Nested Case-Control Study

Carol A. C. Coupland, PhD; Trevor Hill, MSc; Tom Dening, MD; Richard Morriss, MD; Michael Moore, MSc; Julia Hippisley-Cox, MD

A. The General Structure Analysis

The Structure of the Abstract

Subsections	Description	Comment
Introduction	Importance	Raise the question of the study and put forward its objective. **(1) The question** *Anticholinergic medicines have short-term cognitive adverse effects, but it is uncertain whether long-term use of these drugs is associated with an increased risk of dementia.* **(2) The objective** *To assess associations between anticholinergic drug treatments and risk of dementia in persons 55 years or older*
	Objective	

continued

Subsections	Description	Comment
Methods	Design, Setting and Participants	Describe what was used, what was done and how it was done. Provide raw data of the study. (1) The study design (2) The participants selection (3) The exposure to the anticholinergic drugs (4) The confounding variables
	Exposures	
	Main Outcomes and Measures	
Results	Results	Transform the raw data into meaningful results. (1) 63.1% of the study population were women. (2) The adjusted odds ratio for dementia increased, compared with no anticholinergic drug prescriptions in the 1-11 years before the index date. (3) There were significant increases in dementia risk for the several drugs. (4) Associations were stronger in cases diagnosed before the age of 80 years.
Discussion and Conclusion	Conclusions and Relevance	Put forward the answer to the question. (1) Exposure to several types of strong anticholinergic drugs is associated with an increased risk of dementia. (2) The findings highlight the importance of reducing exposure to anticholinergic drugs in middle-aged and older people.

B. The Language Features

Subsections	Description	The Original Abstract	Comment
Introduction	Importance	Anticholinergic medicines ***have*** short-term cognitive adverse effects, ***but it is uncertain whether*** long-term use of these drugs ***is associated*** with an increased risk of dementia.	*It is uncertain whether …* signals the question of the present study. The present tense is used to describe the background of the study: *have, is uncertain, is associated* The aspect of active voice is used to express the point of the experimenters.
	Objective	***To assess*** associations between anticholinergic drug treatments and risk of dementia in persons 55 years or older.	*To assess* signals the objective of the study. This is not a complete sentence.

continued

Subsections	Description	The Original Abstract	Comment
Methods	Design, Setting and Participants	This nested case-control study ***took place*** in general practices in England that contributed to the QResearch primary care database. The study ***evaluated*** whether exposure to anticholinergic drugs was associated with dementia risk in 58 769 patients with a diagnosis of dementia and 225 574 controls 55 years or older matched by age, sex, general practice, and calendar time. Information on prescriptions for 56 drugs with strong anticholinergic properties ***was used*** to calculate measures of cumulative anticholinergic drug exposure. Data ***were analyzed*** from May 2016 to June 2018.	The active voice is used when it stresses the point of the study experimenters: *The study took place, The study evaluated...* The passive voice is used when it stresses the outcomes: *Information... was used, Data were analyzed...* Only the past tense is used in this section.
	Exposures	The primary exposure ***was*** the total standardized daily doses (TSDDs) of anticholinergic drugs prescribed in the 1 to 11 years prior to the date of diagnosis of dementia or equivalent date in matched controls (index date).	The past tense is used in Exposures and Main outcomes: *was*
	Main Outcomes and Measures	Odds ratios (ORs) for dementia associated with cumulative exposure to anticholinergic drugs, for confounding variables.	
Results	Results	Of the entire study population (284 343 case patients and matched controls), 179 365 (63.1%) ***were*** women, and the mean (SD) age of the entire population was 82.2 (6.8) years. The adjusted OR for dementia ***increased*** from 1.06 (95% CI, 1.03-1.09) in the lowest overall anticholinergic exposure category (total exposure of 1-90 TSDDs) to 1.49 (95% CI, 1.44-1.54) in the highest category (>1095 TSDDs), compared with no anticholinergic drug prescriptions in the 1 to 11 years before the index date. There ***were*** significant increases in dementia risk for the anticholinergic antidepressants, ... Associations ***were*** stronger in cases diagnosed before the age of 80 years. The population-attributable fraction associated with total anticholinergic drug exposure during the 1 to 11 years before diagnosis ***was*** 10.3%.	To show the completed actions, the past tense is used in this section: *were, increased, was...*

continued

Subsections	Description	The Original Abstract	Comment
Discussion and Conclusion	Conclusion and Relevance	Exposure to several types of strong anticholinergic drugs ***is associated*** with an increased risk of dementia. These findings ***highlight*** the importance of reducing exposure to anticholinergic drugs in middle-aged and older people.	To show the answer to the questions and implications of the study, the present tense is used: *is associated, highlight...*

3.2 Case 2

Case 2 is a structured abstract from an article titled "Canagliflozin and Renal Outcomes in Type 2 Diabetes and Nephropathy" published on online *The New England Journal of Medicine* (doi: 10.1056/NEJMoa1811744).

The NEW ENGLAND JOURNAL *of* MEDICINE

ESTABLISHED IN 1812 JUNE 13, 2019 VOL. 380 NO. 24

Canagliflozin and Renal Outcomes in Type 2 Diabetes and Nephropathy

V. Perkovic, M.J. Jardine, B. Neal, S. Bompoint, H.J.L. Heerspink, D.M. Charytan, R. Edwards, R. Agarwal, G. Bakris, S. Bull, C.P. Cannon, G. Capuano, P.-L. Chu, D. de Zeeuw, T. Greene, A. Levin, C. Pollock, D.C. Wheeler, Y. Yavin, H. Zhang, B. Zinman, G. Meininger, B.M. Brenner, and K.W. Mahaffey, for the CREDENCE Trial Investigators*

A. The General Structure Analysis

The Structure of the Abstract

Subsections	Description	Comment
Introduction	Background	State the background of the study and put forward its hypothesis. **(1) The background** *Type 2 diabetes mellitus is the leading cause of kidney failure worldwide, but few effective long-term treatments are available.* **(2) The hypothesis** *In cardiovascular trials of inhibitors of sodium–glucose cotransporter 2 (SGLT2), exploratory results have suggested that such drugs may improve renal outcomes in patients with type 2 diabetes.*

continued

Subsections	Description	Comment
Methods	Methods	Describe what was used, what was done and how it was done. Provide raw data of the study. (1) The study design (2) The participants selection (3) The primary outcome (4) The prespecified secondary outcomes
Results	Results	Transform the raw data into meaningful results. (1) 4401 patients had undergone randomization. (2) The relative risk of the primary outcome was 30% lower in the canagliflozin group than in the placebo group. (3) The relative risk of the renal-specific composite of end-stage kidney disease, a doubling of the creatinine level, or death from renal causes was lower by 34%, and the relative risk of end-stage kidney disease was lower by 32%. (4) The canagliflozin group also had a lower risk of cardiovascular death, myocardial infarction, or stroke and hospitalization for heart failure. (5) There were no significant differences in rates of amputation or fracture.
Discussion and Conclusion	Conclusions	Put forward the answer to the question. *In patients with type 2 diabetes and kidney disease, the risk of kidney failure and cardiovascular events was lower in the canagliflozin group than in the placebo group at a median follow-up of 2.62 years.*

B. The Language Features

Subsections	Description	The Original Abstract	Comment
Introduction	Background	Type 2 diabetes mellitus **is** the leading cause of kidney failure worldwide, ***but few*** effective long-term treatments ***are available***. In cardiovascular trials of inhibitors of sodium–glucose cotransporter 2 (SGLT2), ***exploratory results have suggested that such drugs may*** improve renal outcomes in patients with type 2 diabetes.	*..., but few... are available* indicates the unknown of the story. *..., exploratory results have suggested that such drugs may...* states the hypothesis. The present tense is used to describe the background of the study: *is, are* The present perfect tense is used to indicate that the act happening in the past is still existing:

continued

Subsections	Description	The Original Abstract	Comment
			have suggested The modal verb is used to suggest the uncertainty of the hypothesis: *may* The aspect of active voice is used to express the point of the experimenters.
Methods	Methods	In this double-blind, randomized trial, we ***assigned*** patients with type 2 diabetes and albuminuric chronic kidney disease to receive canagliflozin, an oral SGLT2 inhibitor, at a dose of 100 mg daily or placebo. All the patients ***had*** an estimated glomerular filtration rate (GFR) of 30 to <90 ml per minute per 1.73 m^2 of body-surface area and albuminuria (ratio of albumin [mg] to creatinine [g], >300 to 5000) and ***were treated*** with renin–angiotensin system blockade. The primary outcome ***was*** a composite of end-stage kidney disease (dialysis, transplantation, or a sustained estimated GFR of <15 ml per minute per 1.73 m^2), a doubling of the serum creatinine level, or death from renal or cardiovascular causes. Prespecified secondary outcomes ***were*** tested hierarchically.	The active voice is used when it stresses the point of the study experimenters: *We assigned...* The passive voice is used when it stresses the participants selection: *All the patients were treated...* Only the past tense is used in this section.
Results	Results	The trial ***was*** stopped early after a planned interim analysis on the recommendation of the data and safety monitoring committee. At that time, 4401 patients ***had*** undergone randomization, with a median follow-up of 2.62 years. The relative risk of the primary outcome ***was*** 30% lower in the canagliflozin group than in the placebo group, with event rates of 43.2 and 61.2 per 1000 patient-years, respectively (hazard ratio, 0.70; 95% confidence interval [CI], 0.59 to 0.82; P=0.00001). The relative risk of the renal-specific composite of end-stage kidney disease, a doubling of the creatinine level, or death from renal causes ***was*** lower by 34% (hazard ratio, 0.66; 95% CI, 0.53 to 0.81; P<0.001), and the relative risk of	To show the completed actions, the past tense is used in this section: *was, had...*

continued

Subsections	Description	The Original Abstract	Comment
		end-stage kidney disease was lower by 32% (hazard ratio, 0.68; 95% CI, 0.54 to 0.86; P = 0.002). The canagliflozin group also ***had*** a lower risk of cardiovascular death, myocardial infarction, or stroke (hazard ratio, 0.80; 95% CI, 0.67 to 0.95; P=0.01) and hospitalization for heart failure (hazard ratio, 0.61; 95% CI, 0.47 to 0.80; P < 0.001). There ***were*** no significant differences in rates of amputation or fracture.	
Discussion and Conclusion	Conclusions	In patients with type 2 diabetes and kidney disease, the risk of kidney failure and cardiovascular events ***was*** lower in the canagliflozin group than in the placebo group at a median follow-up of 2.62 years.	The past tense is used to show the answer to the questions, which was revealed in the past during the experiment: *was*...

3.3 Case 3

Case 3 is a structured abstract from the article titled "Type and timing of menopausal hormone therapy and breast cancer risk: individual participant meta-analysis of the worldwide epidemiological evidence" published on *The Lancet* (doi: 10.1016/S0140-6736 (19)31709-X).

Type and timing of menopausal hormone therapy and breast cancer risk: individual participant meta-analysis of the worldwide epidemiological evidence

CrossMark

*Collaborative Group on Hormonal Factors in Breast Cancer**

oa OPEN ACCESS

A. The General Structure Analysis

The Structure of the Abstract

Subsections	Description	Comment
Introduction	Background	State the question and put forward its objective. **(1) The question** *Published findings on breast cancer risk associated with different types of menopausal hormone therapy (MHT) are inconsistent, with limited information on long-term effects.* **(2) The objective** *We bring together the epidemiological evidence, published and unpublished, on these associations, and review the relevant randomised evidence.*
Methods	Methods	Describe what was used, what was done and how it was done. Provide data of the study. (1) Participants selection (2) Study identification (3) Data collection (4) Statistical analyses
Results	Findings	Transform the data into meaningful results. (1) During prospective follow-up, 108 647 postmenopausal women developed breast cancer at mean age 65 years and 51% had used MHT. (2) Among women with complete information, mean MHT duration was 10 years in current users and 7 years in past users. (3) Every MHT type, except vaginal oestrogens, was associated with excess breast cancer risks, which were greater for oestrogen-progestagen than oestrogen-only preparations. (4) Among current users, these excess risks were definite even during years 1–4, and were twice as great during years 5–14. The oestrogen-progestagen risks during years 5–14 were greater with daily than with less frequent progestagen use. (5) For a given preparation, the RRs during years 5–14 of current use were much greater for oestrogen-receptor-positive tumours than for oestrogen-receptor-negative tumours, were similar for women starting MHT at ages 40–44, 45–49, 50–54, and 55–59 years, and were attenuated by starting after age 60 years or by adiposity. (6) After ceasing MHT, some excess risk persisted for more than 10 years; its magnitude depended on the duration of previous use.
Discussion and Conclusion	Interpretation	Put forward the answer to the question. (1) *If these associations are largely causal, then for women of average weight in developed countries, 5 years of MHT, starting at age 50 years, would increase breast cancer incidence at ages 50–69 years by about one in every 50 users of oestrogen plus daily progestagen preparations; one in every 70 users of oestrogen plus intermittent progestagen preparations; and one in every 200 users of oestrogen-only preparations.* (2) *The corresponding excesses from 10 years of MHT would be about twice as great.*

B. The Language Features

Subsections	Description	The Original Abstract	Comment
Introduction	Background	Published findings on breast cancer risk associated with different types of menopausal hormone therapy (MHT) ***are inconsistent, with limited information on long-term effects***. We ***bring together*** the epidemiological evidence, published and unpublished, on these associations, and ***review*** the relevant randomised evidence.	*... are inconsistent, with limited information on long-term effects* signals the question of the present study. *We bring together... and review...* signals the objective of the study. The present tense is used to describe the background and the objective of the study: *are, bring together, review* The aspect of active voice is used to express the point of the researchers.
Methods	Methods	Principal analyses ***used*** individual participant data from all eligible prospective studies that had sought information on the type and timing of MHT use; the main analyses ***are*** of individuals with complete information on this. Studies ***were identified*** by searching many formal and informal sources regularly from Jan 1, 1992, to Jan 1, 2018. Current users ***were included*** up to 5 years (mean 1.4 years) after last-reported MHT use. Logistic regression ***yielded*** adjusted risk ratios (RRs) comparing particular groups of MHT users versus never users.	The active voice is used when it stresses the point of the researchers: *Principal analyses used...* The passive voice is used when it stresses the study identification: *Studies were identified...* The past tense is generally used to indicate the completed actions: *used, were, yielded* But the present tense is used to indicate the principle of the Methods: *The main analyses are of individuals...*
Results	Findings	During prospective follow-up, 108 647 postmenopausal women ***developed*** breast cancer at mean age 65 years (SD 7); 55 575 (51%) ***had used*** MHT. Among women with complete information, mean MHT duration was 10 years (SD 6) in current users ... Among current users, these excess risks ***were*** definite even during years 1–4, and ***were*** twice as great	To indicate the completed actions, the past tense is used in this section: *developed, was, increased, were, persisted, depended ...*

continued

Subsections	Description	The Original Abstract	Comment
		during years 5–14; oestrogen-only RR 1.33, 1.28–1.37). The oestrogen-progestagen risks during years 5–14 ***were*** greater with daily than with less frequent progestagen use. For a given preparation, the RRs during years 5–14 of current use ***were*** much greater for oestrogen-receptor-positive tumours than for oestrogen-receptor-negative tumours ... After ceasing MHT, some excess risk ***persisted*** for more than 10 years; its magnitude ***depended*** on the duration of previous use, with little excess following less than 1 year of MHT use.	To express the actions in the past before another action in the past, the past perfect tense is used: *had used*
Discussion and Conclusion	Interpretation	If these associations are largely causal, then for women of average weight in developed countries, 5 years of MHT, starting at age 50 years, ***would increase*** breast cancer incidence at ages 50–69 years ... The corresponding excesses from 10 years of MHT ***would be*** about twice as great.	To show the answer to the questions and implications of the study, the modal verb is used: *would increase, would be*

4. Key Points

- The abstract should have the same structure as the paper: hypothesis, methods, results and answer.
- The writer should prepare abstract in accordance with formatting guidelines specified by the journals.
- The abstract must be complete, informative, coherent and consistent with the whole text.
- The abstract should be condensed and concise in order to clearly present the information with as few words as possible.

5. Revision Exercise

Direction: The following paragraph needs revision before being used as an abstract. After revising the paragraph, change it into a format that would be acceptable for a journal that requires structured abstracts.

It is known that retirement can increase mortality in men, we hypothesized that retirement can increase mortality in professional women who have spent 30 or more years in the work force. To test this hypothesis, we compared the mortality rate between 200 women who remained in the work force past the age of retirement with 200 women who retired at the age of 65. We found that after adjusting for other health factors, the mortality rate was higher in the retired professionals. We speculate that the crucial variable leading to an increase in mortality is attachment to career, not gender. Retirement can increase mortality in professional women who have spent 30 or more years in the work force.

1. Which section of a research paper would include this paragraph?
2. What is/are the independent variable (s)?
3. What is/are the dependent variable (s)?
4. What is the population?
5. Point out one organization change that you would make.
6. Write a message/phrase title for this paper.

Chapter Thirteen Citations and References

1. The Function of Citations and References

At one level the function of **a CITATION** is to give credit for the words or ideas of others, and the function of **a REFERENCE** is to direct the reader to the source of these words or ideas. However, at a level more relevant to the writing of a scientific paper, **the function of a citation or reference** is to supply outside support for the foundation on which the present research is based. To fulfill this function, only the best and most recent sources should usually be cited. Quality, not quantity, is the goal when choosing outside support. Always remember that interested readers will be provided with further references after reading the referenced paper from the present study. For this reason, review papers are sometimes a good choice for a reference paper. Writers should never include an internal citation without a corresponding reference, or a reference without a corresponding internal citation, and should never cite or reference a manuscript or portion of a manuscript that has not been read.

2. The Structure of Citations and References

Different journals require different formatting citations and references, and most journals provide a web page that outlines the requirements. If not, then a quick look at a recent edition of the journal should provide the necessary information for formatting the citations and reference page.

Medical journals often require references to be numerically sequenced by order of mention. *The Uniform Requirements for Manuscripts Submitted to Biomedical Journals* document available at www.icmje.org/ provides requirements and examples for several major international journals.

3. A Few Words about Names

To properly cite and reference outside material, the writer must be able to recognize and sequence family names, given names and initials. This can sometimes be a challenge when citing an unfamiliar foreign name. A little internet research can be very helpful in the editing process to avoid making any embarrassing mistakes with the names of cited researchers. Transcribing names from a character to a letter-based system requires some special skill. Again, a little internet research should be enough to make certain that the name has been transcribed in a way that accords with that author's other writings. The key for any individual writer is to try to make certain that the name has been transcribed consistently throughout the writer's body of works. Phonetic symbols such as the ***Lv spelling*** of some Chinese names is unrecognizable to the majority of western readers and should probably be avoided.

4. Key Points

- Review papers are a good choice for referring readers to relevant background information and support.
- Never include a reference that has not been cited within the paper.
- Never include a reference that has not been read.

5. Revision Exercise

Direction: Do an internet search and then format the following according to the criteria for the journal, *Nature* and *Cell.*

Authors Name: T. Wakayama, A. C. Perry, M. Zuccotti, K. R. Johnson, K. R., R. Yanagimachi

Paper Name: Full-term development of mice from enucleated oocytes injected with cumulus cell nuclei

Journal Name: *Nature*

Year Published: 1998

Issue Number: 394

Page Numbers: 369–374

Authors Name: K. Takahashi, S. Yamanaka

Paper Name: Induction of pluripotent stem cells from mouse embryonic and adult fibroblast cultures by defined factors

Journal Name: *Cell*

Publication Year: 2006

Issue Number: 126

Page Numbers: 663–676

Chapter Fourteen Figures and Tables

The function of **FIGURES** and **TABLES** is to provide the data, photographs and statistical information accumulated during the study in a clear and compact format. The proper use of **figures** and **tables** allows the authors to concentrate on results in the text of the paper and to keep raw data in the background through citations to the figures and tables. The specific format required for **figures** and **tables** may vary from publication to publication; so the specific requirements must be read and followed for the specific publication in question, including requirements for table and figure legends.

1. Introduction to the Figures

As a visual presentation of results, the figure presents data in a clear, compact and organized way. Authors need to be aware of the different purposes of statements, figures and tables. If simple statements could clarify the results, it is not necessary to use figures; figures are more suitable for presenting pronounced trends rather than static or exact numbers. Most figures that present quantitative information have at least **seven elements: figure number, figure caption/legend, data field, vertical scale, horizontal scale, labels and data** (Figure 1).

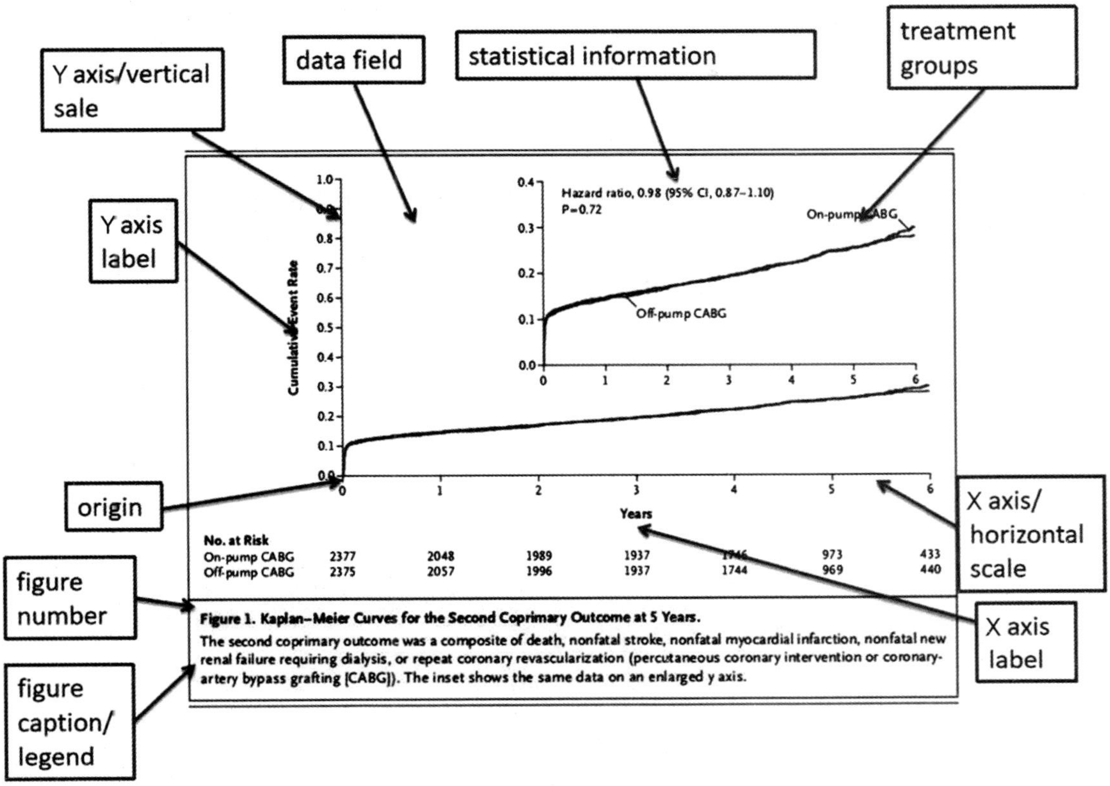

Figure 1 Components of the Figure

2. Cases of the Figures

The cases in this part are from ***the Lancet, NEJM, JAMA*** and ***BMJ***, showing how the four major types of figures—***diagrams, bar graphs, scatter plots*** and ***line graphs***—are designed and referred to in the texts.

(1) Diagram

Diagram, containing only text, is a type of non-statistical figure and mostly used for describing steps of a procedure or summarizing guidelines, thus clarifying or amplifying the methods of a study. It is usually used to describe how participants were selected or how studies were collected.

Case 1

Case 1 is from "Clinical presentation, treatment, and short-term outcomes of lung injury associated with e-cigarettes or vaping: a prospective observational cohort study” published on *The Lancet* (doi.org/10.1016/ S0140-6736 (19)32679-0).

Clinical presentation, treatment, and short-term outcomes of lung injury associated with e-cigarettes or vaping: a prospective observational cohort study

CrossMark

Denitza P Blagev, Dixie Harris*, Angela C Dunn, David W Guidry, Colin K Grissom, Michael J Lanspa*

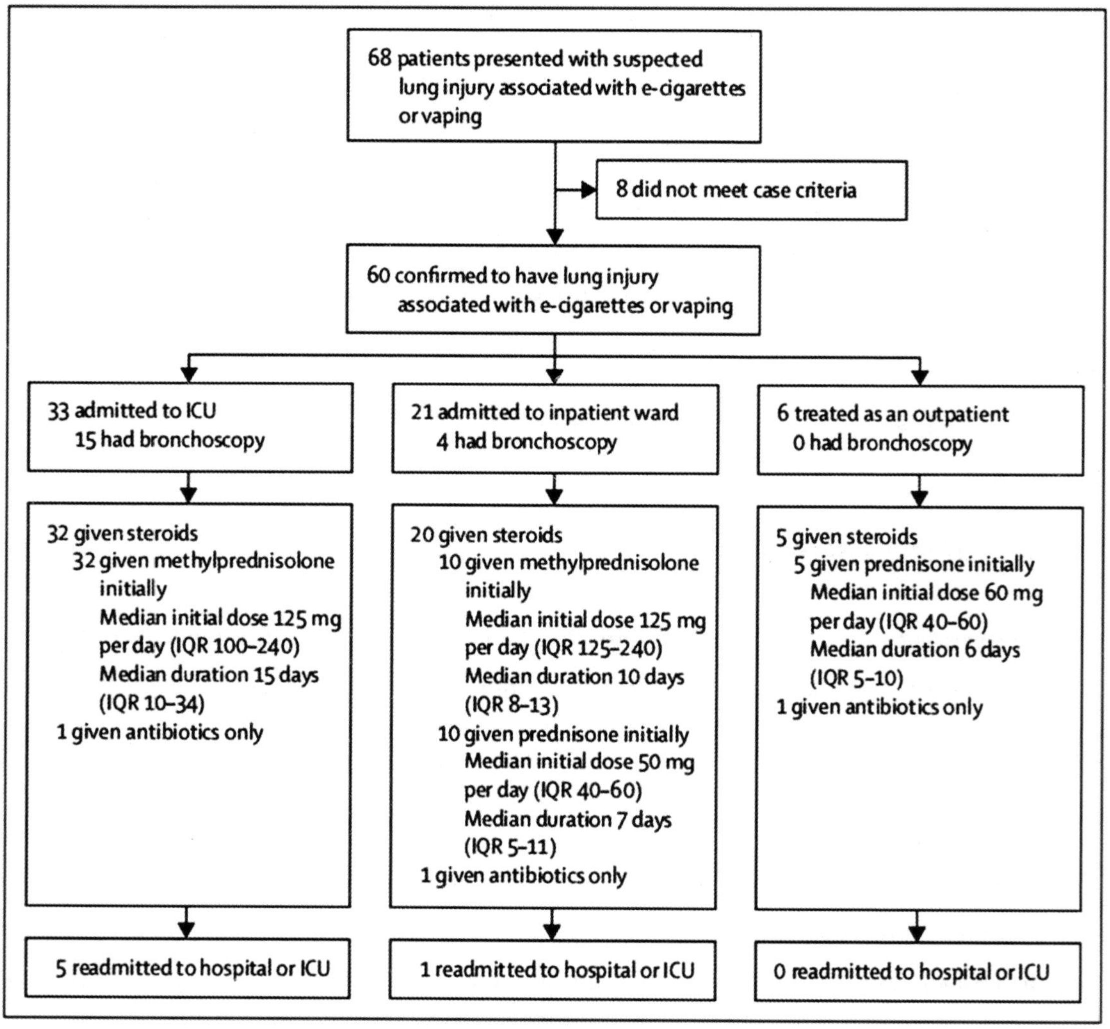

Figure 1: Screening, admittance, and treatment of patients with lung injury associated with e-cigarettes or vaping
ICU=intensive care unit.

In the text, the authors describe that *"68 patients with suspected lung injury associated with e-cigarettes or vaping were referred to the task force. On review, eight patients did not meet the case definition and were excluded. Thus, 60 patients with confirmed lung injury associated with e-cigarettes or vaping, who presented to 13 hospitals or outpatient clinics in the integrated health system, were included in this analysis (Figure 1)*."

In the Results section, the authors are not expected to report data both in the text and in figures/tables, but important data can be emphasized. Here authors report the total number of patients referred (68), those excluded (8) and finally included (60) in the text, and at the same time refer readers to the diagram for further detailed information by means of a parenthesis. Only data related to the sample size of the study is given in the text.

This diagram describes how patients with lung injury associated with e-cigarettes or vaping were screened, admitted to hospital and treated in this cohort study. This diagram is **effective** due to the following features:

1) The layout is easy to read, and the size of letters and symbols are carefully chosen to withstand photographic reduction to column or page width in the printed journal;

2) The title goes above while legend comes below the figure;

3) The text in the boxes gives clear description to the participants and treatments they underwent in detail: type of medicine, dose and duration. These descriptions are mostly in the phrase structure of "N + past participle";

4) The consistency is achieved through the use of identical sentence structures in parallel boxes;

5) The sample sizes are consistent with those reported in the text;

6) The acronyms (ICU) explained in the legend ensure that the figure could be understood independent of the text.

Case 2

Case 2 is from the article titled "A Randomized Trial of E-Cigarettes versus Nicotine-Replacement Therapy" published on *The New England Journal of Medicine* (doi: 10.1016/ S0140-6736 (19)32679-0).

The NEW ENGLAND JOURNAL *of* MEDICINE

ORIGINAL ARTICLE

A Randomized Trial of E-Cigarettes versus Nicotine-Replacement Therapy

Peter Hajek, Ph.D., Anna Phillips-Waller, B.Sc., Dunja Przulj, Ph.D., Francesca Pesola, Ph.D., Katie Myers Smith, D.Psych., Natalie Bisal, M.Sc., Jinshuo Li, M.Phil., Steve Parrott, M.Sc., Peter Sasieni, Ph.D., Lynne Dawkins, Ph.D., Louise Ross, Maciej Goniewicz, Ph.D., Pharm.D., Qi Wu, M.Sc., and Hayden J. McRobbie, Ph.D.

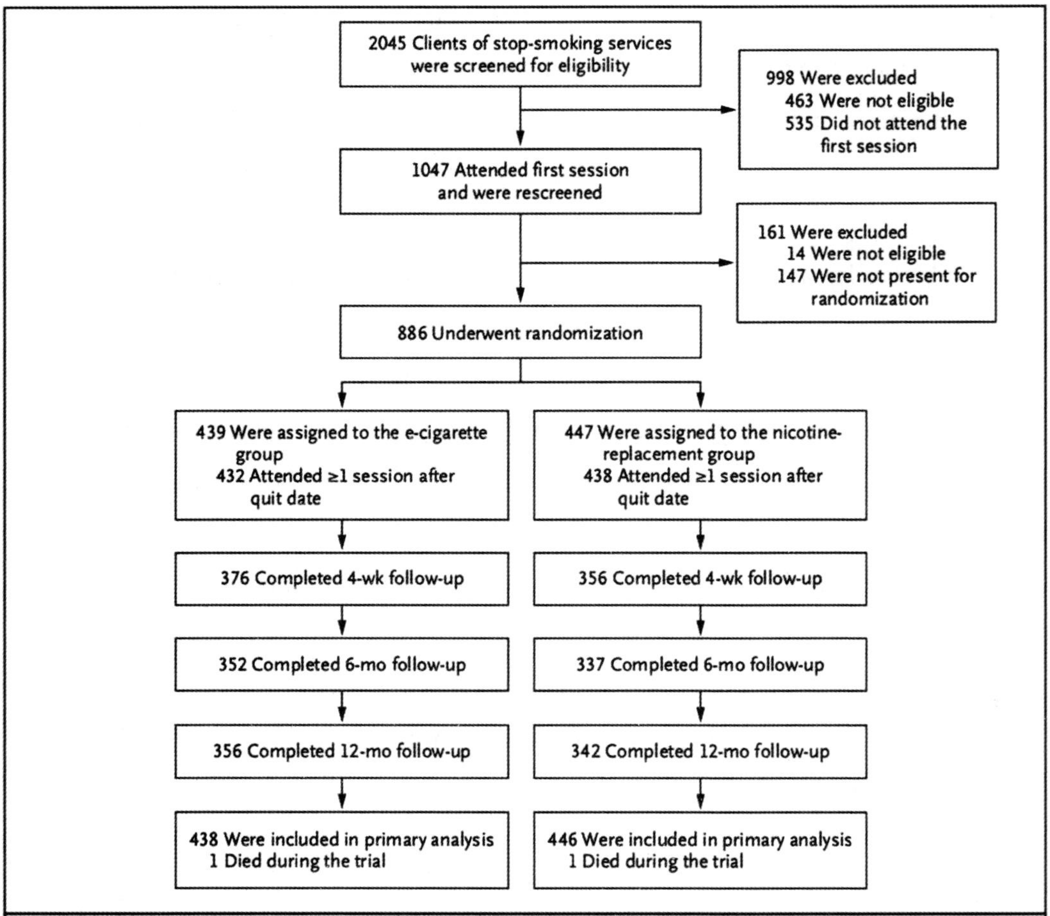

Figure 1. Screening, Randomization, and Follow-up.
Reasons for ineligibility in 463 of the 2045 persons screened are detailed in Table S11 in the Supplementary Appendix. Of the 438 participants in the e-cigarette group who were included in the primary analysis, 3 stopped treatment and declined follow-up and 13 stopped treatment and permitted follow-up. Of the 446 participants in the nicotine-replacement group who were included in the primary analysis, 5 stopped treatment and declined follow-up and 36 stopped treatment and permitted follow-up.

This diagram describes the procedures by sentences or phrases to keep consistent flow of the data. It can be seen that the authors report the total number of patients screened and randomized (with descriptions of number of patients in the e-cigarette group and nicotine-replacement group respectively) in the text.

..."A total of 2045 clients of stop-smoking services were screened, and 886 underwent randomization (439 to the e-cigarette group and 447 to the nicotine-replacement group). Of the randomly assigned participants, 78.8% completed the 52- week follow-up (Fig. 1)."...

Also in the legends of the diagram, the authors refer readers to supplementary appendix for reasons for ineligibility. They also describe further experimental details concerning participants in each group. These ensure the diagram to be understood independent of the text.

(2) Graphs

Graphs are suitable for presenting relationships whereas non-statistical figures, which visually present information that does not contain data, are used to confirm findings or provide explanatory information. In other words, they serve to present evidence that supports the results. In statistical figures, selecting a graphical format (including bar graph, line graph, and scatterplot) is done according to the type of relationship that the authors wish to communicate; for example, line graphs are appropriate for showing trends and bar graphs for magnitudes.

Bar graphs are used when the authors wish to compare the value of a single variable (usually a summary value such as a mean) among several groups. For example, a bar graph is appropriate to show the mean size of plants harvested from plots that received 4 different fertilizer treatments. (Note that although a bar graph might be used to show differences between only 2 groups, especially for pedagogical purposes, editors of many journals would prefer that authors save space by presenting such information in the text.)

A. Bar Graph

Case 3

Case 3 is from the article titled "Ibrutinib and Venetoclax for first-line treatment of CLL" published on *The New England Journal of Medicine* (doi: 10.1056/NEJMoa1900574).

The NEW ENGLAND JOURNAL of MEDICINE

ESTABLISHED IN 1812 MAY 30, 2019 VOL. 380 NO. 22

Ibrutinib and Venetoclax for First-Line Treatment of CLL

Nitin Jain, M.D., Michael Keating, M.D., Philip Thompson, M.D., Alessandra Ferrajoli, M.D., Jan Burger, M.D., Ph.D., Gautam Borthakur, M.D., Koichi Takahashi, M.D., Zeev Estrov, M.D., Nathan Fowler, M.D., Tapan Kadia, M.D., Marina Konopleva, M.D., Ph.D., Yesid Alvarado, M.D., Musa Yilmaz, M.D., Courtney DiNardo, M.D., Prithviraj Bose, M.D., Maro Ohanian, D.O., Naveen Pemmaraju, M.D., Elias Jabbour, M.D., Koji Sasaki, M.D., Rashmi Kanagal-Shamanna, M.D., Keyur Patel, M.D., Ph.D., Jeffrey Jorgensen, M.D., Ph.D., Naveen Garg, M.D., Xuemei Wang, M.S., Katrina Sondermann, B.A., Nichole Cruz, R.N., Chongjuan Wei, Ph.D., Ana Ayala, R.N., William Plunkett, Ph.D., Hagop Kantarjian, M.D., Varsha Gandhi, Ph.D., and William Wierda, M.D., Ph.D.

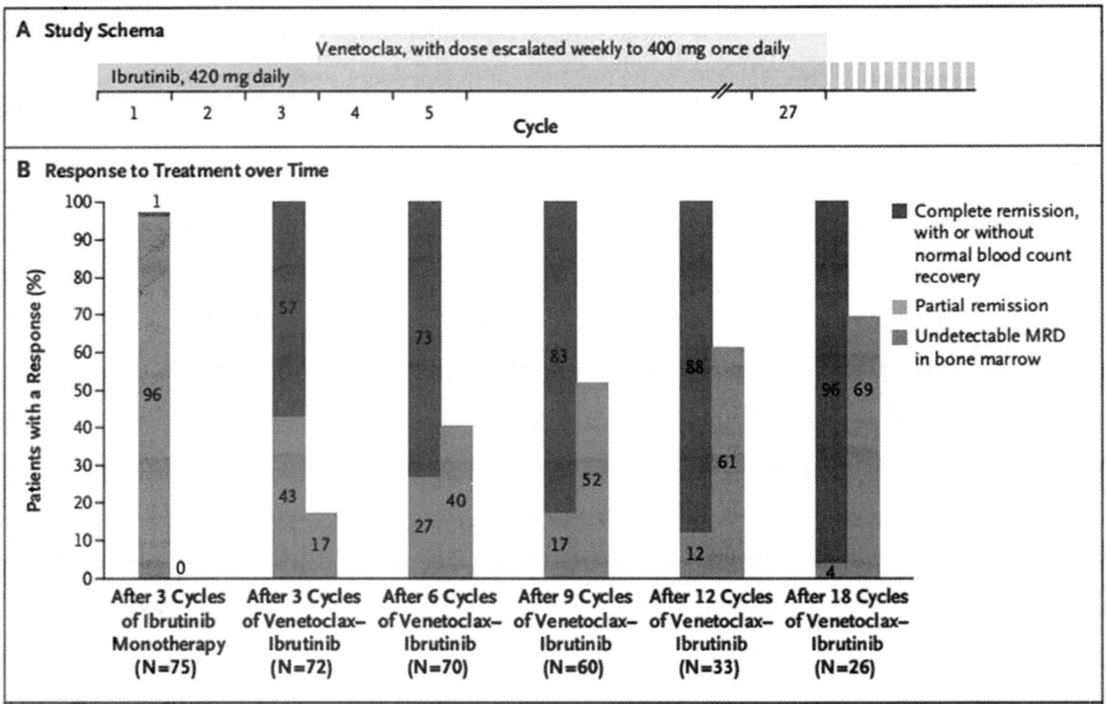

Figure 1. Study Schema and Response to Treatment.

Panel A shows the study schema. Patients received ibrutinib monotherapy (420 mg once daily) for 3 cycles (each cycle was 28 days), and then venetoclax was added. The dose of venetoclax was escalated weekly to a target dose of 400 mg once daily. Combined ibrutinib and venetoclax were administered for a total of 24 cycles. Patients who remained positive for minimal residual disease (MRD) in bone marrow at the end of combined treatment could continue ibrutinib alone until disease progression or unacceptable toxic effects. Clinical responses and MRD were measured after 3 cycles of ibrutinib monotherapy and then after every 3 cycles for the first 12 cycles of the combination and every 6 cycles for cycles 13 to 24 of the combination. Panel B shows response to treatment over time. Responses (complete remission, with or without normal blood count recovery; partial remission; and undetectable MRD in bone marrow) are shown for patients after 3 cycles of ibrutinib monotherapy and at different time points for the combination therapy.

This is a composite figure including two panels: A and B. The two are both signaled with a brief title, and demarcated with a line in between. Composite figures are placed vertically rather than horizontally. Title of the composite figure should include description of both panels. In addition, the figure legends should give details concerning both individual figures, as is clearly illustrated in this example.

In the text, the authors report in the Results section:

... *"Responses are shown in Figure 1B, and in Table S2 in the Supplementary Appendix. After the initial 3 cycles of ibrutinib monotherapy, most responses were partial. After the addition of venetoclax, the proportions of patients who had complete remission or complete remission with incomplete count recovery and remission with undetectable minimal residual disease in bone marrow increased over time (Fig. 1B, and Fig. S1 in the Supplementary Appendix)."* ...

The description of this figure is well done in this text. The authors did not repeat any data in the figure, but acutely pointed out the trend shown by the figure: Most responses were partial after the monotherapy, and the proportions of patients who were showing recovery increased over time with the use of combination therapy. Actually, readers are not expected to interpret the figures themselves. Therefore, the most outstanding features reflected in the figures should be summarized and highlighted in the text. This figure is effective due to the following features:

1) The measured variable is labeled on the Y axis (patients with a response) with units given (%);

2) The categorical variable (different time points of the treatment: cycles + medicine) is labeled on the X axis, with the sample size, and each category is designated;

3) A second categorical variable (complete remission, with or without normal blood count recovery; partial remission; and undetectable MRD in bone marrow) within responses has been designated by different bar fill color. The bar colors are defined in a key, located within the graph; the colors allow clear distinctions to be made between datasets;

4) The legend explains the time for the measurements of patient responses;

5) In the legend, the present tense is used for describing the figure while the past tense is used to describe procedures;

6) A period follows "Figure 1" and the legend itself; "Figure" is not abbreviated.

B. Line graph

Line graphs plot a series of related values that depict a change in Y as a function of X. Two common examples are a growth curve for an individual or population over time, and a dose-response curve showing effects of increasing doses of a drug or treatment.

Case 4

Case 4 is from the article titled "Prevalence of cervical disease at age 20 after immunisation with bivalent HPV vaccine at age 12-13 in Scotland: retrospective population study" published on *British Medical Journal* (doi: 10.1136/bmj.l1161).

RESEARCH

OPEN ACCESS

Check for updates

Prevalence of cervical disease at age 20 after immunisation with bivalent HPV vaccine at age 12-13 in Scotland: retrospective population study

Tim Palmer,[1] Lynn Wallace,[2] Kevin G Pollock,[3,4] Kate Cuschieri,[5] Chris Robertson,[3,6,7] Kim Kavanagh,[7] Margaret Cruickshank[8]

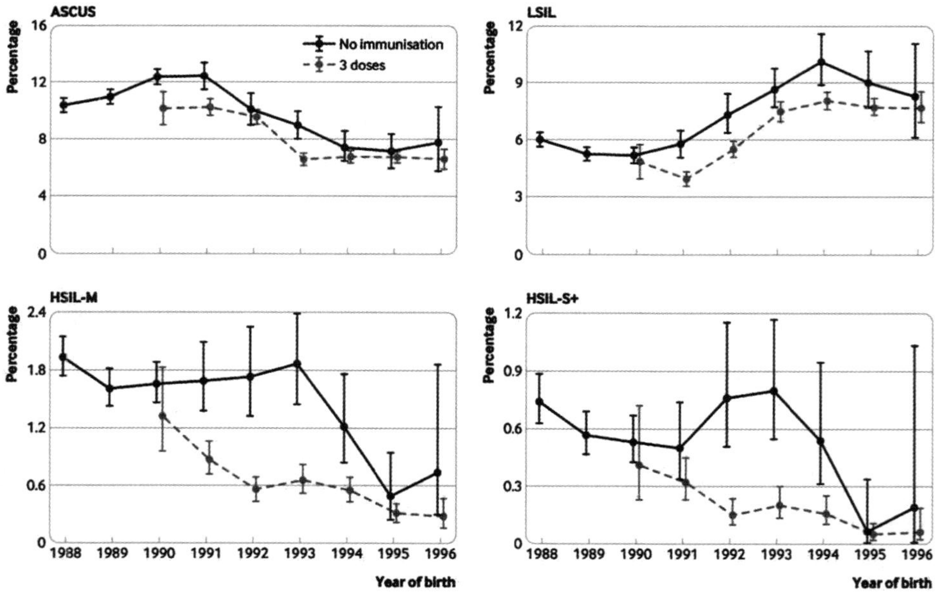

Fig 2 | Cytological abnormality (% of women screened) by year of birth and immunisation status. 1988-90=pre-immunisation programme cohort; 1991-94=catch-up cohort; 1995-96=routinely immunised cohort. Whiskers represent 95% confidence intervals. ASCUS=atypical squamous cells of undetermined significance; LSIL=low grade squamous intraepithelial lesion; HSIL=high grade squamous intraepithelial lesion (HSIL-M=mild dyskaryosis; HSIL-S+=severe dyskaryosis)

Table 2 | Number (percentage) of records in data extract stratified by year of birth, number of doses of bivalent human papillomavirus vaccine, cytological abnormality, referral for colposcopy, and histological diagnosis

	Year of birth									
Variables	**1988**	**1989**	**1990**	**1991**	**1992**	**1993**	**1994**	**1995**	**1996**	**Total**
No of records	17589	16801	17471	17618	16669	16050	15854	15229	5414	138692
Vaccine doses:										
0	17579 (99.9)	16731 (99.6)	14038 (80.4)	4994 (28.3)	3002 (20.3)	3283 (20.3)	2209 (13.9)	1665 (10.9)	545 (10.1)	64026 (46.2)
1	3 (0.02)	22 (0.1)	233 (1.4)	538 (3.1)	415 (2.5)	437 (2.7)	267 (1.7)	101 (0.7)	29 (0.5)	2051 (1.5)
2	2 (0.01)	18 (0.1)	488 (2.8)	1196 (6.8)	815 (5.1)	833 (5.2)	548 (3.5)	161 (1.1)	38 (0.7)	4135 (3.0)
3	5 (0.03)	30 (0 2)	2706 (15.5)	10890 (61.8)	12401 (74.4)	11517 (71.8)	12830 (80.9)	13229 (87.3)	4802 (88.7)	68480 (49.4)
Cytology result:										
Negative	14500 (82.4)	13923 (82.9)	14302 (81.9)	14780 (83.9)	14031 (84.2)	13640 (85.0)	13452 (84.8)	13080 (85.9)	4656 (86.0)	116364 (83.9)
Borderline/ASCUS	1819 (10.3)	1828 (10.9)	2102 (12.0)	1939 (11.0)	1624 (9.8)	1143 (7.1)	1112 (7.0)	1034 (6.8)	365 (6.7)	12966 (9.3)
Low grade dyskaryosis/LSIL	929 (5.3)	779 (4.6)	786 (4.5)	694 (3.9)	869 (5.2)	1111 (6.9	1178 (7.4)	1061 (7.0)	375 (6.9)	7782 (5.6)
HSIL-M	208 (1.2)	176 (1.0)	191 (1.1)	137 (0.8)	93 (0.6)	102 (0.6)	76 (0.5)	43 (0.3)	13 (0.2)	1040 (0.7)
HSIL-S+	132 (0.8)	95 (0.6)	90 (0.5)	68 (0.4)	52 (0.3)	54 (0.4)	36 (0.2)	8 (0.1)	5 (0.1)	540 (0.4)
Referral for colposcopy	680 (3.9)	612 (3.6)	557 (3.2)	434 (2.5)	355 (2.1)	295 (1.9)	278 (1.7)	120 (0.8)	20 (0.4)	3351 (2.4)
Histological diagnosis:										
CIN grade 1	122 (0.7)	102 (0.6)	98 (0.6)	76 (0.4)	63 (0.4)	60 (0.4)	45 (0.3)	26 (0.2)	4 (0.1)	596 (.4)
CIN grade 2	151 (0.9)	118 (0.7)	106 (0.6)	75 (0.4)	64 (0.4)	63 (0.4)	38 (0.2)	20 (0.1)	2 (0.04)	637 (0.5)
CIN grade 3 or worse	103 (0.6)	81 (0.5)	86 (0.5)	66 (0.4)	53 (0.3)	38 (0.2)	29 (0.2)	9 (0.1)	4 (0.1)	469 (0.3)

ASCUS=atypical squamous cells of undetermined significance; LSIL=low grade squamous intraepithelial lesion; HSIL=high grade squamous intraepithelial lesion (HSIL-M=mild dyskaryosis; HSIL-S+=severe dyskaryosis); CIN=cervical intraepithelial neoplasia.

This figure is reported in the "cytological outcomes" subsection in the Results section. Rates of severe and moderate dyskaryosis in unvaccinated compared with fully vaccinated women born in 1995 and 1996 **were not significantly different** (Figure 2). Overall, borderline/ASCUS rates declined by 34% (30% to 39%), with a similar trend over the cohort in vaccinated and unvaccinated women (interaction test $P = 0.11$), although the rate was lower in vaccinated women (15%, 11% to 19%). The reporting of low grade dyskaryosis/LSIL increased during the period of observation. **The trend** with birth cohort was the same for vaccinated and unvaccinated women (interaction test $P = 0.17$); vaccinated women had 19% (14% to 24%) lower rates (Table 2 and Figure 2). The text combines description of both figures and tables, with trends and relationships from figures, and exact numbers from tables. The figures and tables are effective due to the features:

1) The title in the form of noun phrase + preposition phrase, specifying the two variables (year of birth and immunization status), clearly conveys the content of the figure;

2) Different symbols (types and colors of lines) are used to distinguish immunization status;

3) The key to the symbols is placed in the body of the graph where space permits. Symbols are large enough to be easily recognizable in the final graph size;

4) How different years of birth fits into the cohorts is clearly described in the legend;

5) Whiskers are plotted for each point and defined in the legend as well;

6) Abbreviations are explained in the legend;

7) Each plot in the compound figure is signaled with a keyword;

8) The title of this figure is given at the top, which is according to the style of this specific journal.

C. Scatterplots

X, Y Scatterplots are plots of X, Y coordinates showing each individual's or sample's score on two variables. When plotting data this way authors are usually interested in knowing whether the two variables show a "relationship", i.e. Do they change in value together in a consistent way? When one variable is clearly dependent upon another (e.g. height depends on age, but it is hard to imagine age depending on height), the convention is to plot the dependent variable on the Y axis and the independent variable on the X axis.

Case 5

Case 5 is from the article titled "Diagnostic Performance of Creatinine-Based Equations for Estimating Glomerular Filtration Rate in Adults 65 Years and Older" published on *JAMA Internal Medicine* (doi: 10.1001/jamainternmed.2019.0223).

Research

JAMA Internal Medicine | Original Investigation

Diagnostic Performance of Creatinine-Based Equations for Estimating Glomerular Filtration Rate in Adults 65 Years and Older

Luciano da Silva Selistre, MD, PhD; Dener L. Rech, MD, MS; Vandréa de Souza, MD, PhD; Jean Iwaz, PhD; Sandrine Lemoine, MD, PhD; Laurence Dubourg, MD, PhD

Figure 2. Chronic Kidney Disease Epidemiology Collaboration Equation Scatter Plots of Equation-Estimated Glomerular Filtration Rates in Function of Inulin-Measured Glomerular Filtration Rates in the Whole Population

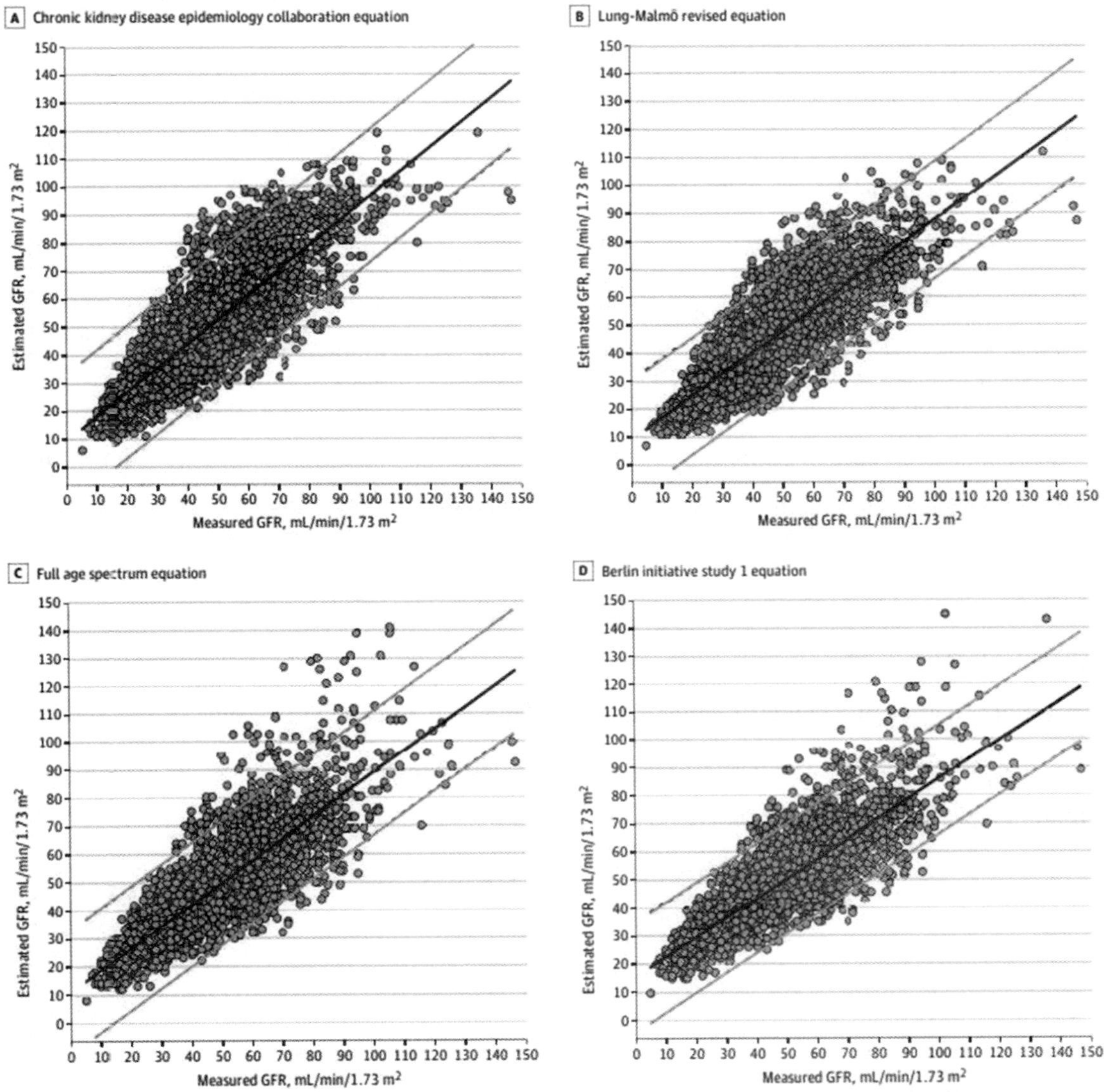

The solid line represents the regression line. The dotted lines represent the 95% limits of prediction. The concordance correlation coefficient (CCC) for panel A is 0.832 (95% CI, 0.827-0.838); B, 0.838 (95% CI, 0.832-0.843); C, 0.817 (95% CI, 0.812-0.823); D, 0.826 (95% CI, 0.820-0.832).

This study aims to evaluate the performance of four plasma creatinine–based equations:

...the classic CKD-EPI vs Full Age Spectrum (FAS), Lund-Malmö Revised (LMR), and Berlin Initiative Study (BIS 1), and compare the equation- estimated GFRs with measured GFRs (by inulin clearance) in older adults of different age groups and different CKD levels...

This figure is reported in the "Concordance Correlation Coefficient" subsection in the Results section. The authors generalized from the data and pointed out that no CCC was greater than 0.9, and identified the equation that had the lowest CCC, thus providing interpretation instead of repetition of the data.

"In the whole population and in all subgroups, no CCC between measured GFR and estimated GFR by any equation was greater than 0.900. BIS 1 had the lowest CCC in the whole cohort and in participants aged 65 to 75 years (Figure 2)."

This Figure 2 *"Chronic Kidney Disease Epidemiology Collaboration Equation Scatter Plots of Equation-Estimated Glomerular Filtration Rates in Function of Inulin-Measured Glomerular Filtration Rates in the Whole Population"* is effective due to the following features:

1) The title in the form of noun phrase + prep phrase is informative and concise;

2) Each axis is labeled (including units where appropriate) and includes numbered and minor ticks to allow easy determination of the values of plotted points;

3) The sample size is specified in the title;

4) The regression line is plotted on the graph to indicate the relationship between the variables; explanations of the lines are given in the figure legend; statistical significance (Concordance Correlation Coefficient including confidence intervals) is also given in the legend;

5) The range of each axis has been carefully selected to maximize the spread of the points and to minimize wasted blank space where no points fall;

6) The styles are consistent between plots in the composite figure.

3. Introduction to the Tables

The **Tables** present lists of numbers or text in columns, each column having a title or label. In research papers, they serve to provide characteristics of participants or present data that support the results. They are used to organize data that are too detailed or complicated to be described adequately in the text, allowing the readers to quickly see the results.

The **Tables** mostly include **four parts: the legend, column headings, the body, and footnotes** (Figure 2).

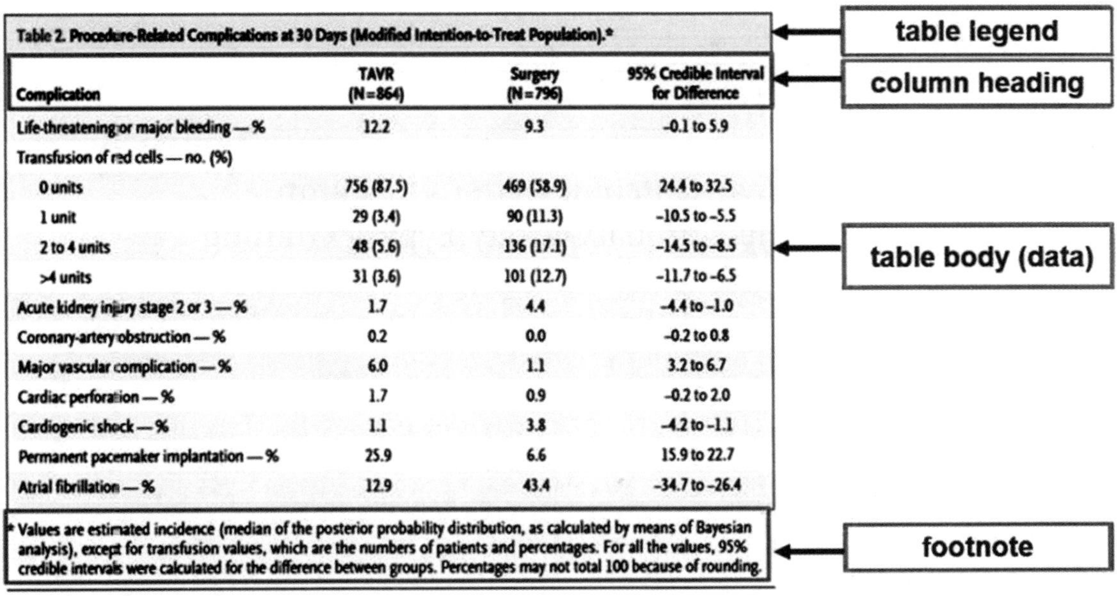

Table 2. Procedure-Related Complications at 30 Days (Modified Intention-to-Treat Population).*

Complication	TAVR (N=864)	Surgery (N=796)	95% Credible Interval for Difference
Life-threatening or major bleeding — %	12.2	9.3	-0.1 to 5.9
Transfusion of red cells — no. (%)			
0 units	756 (87.5)	469 (58.9)	24.4 to 32.5
1 unit	29 (3.4)	90 (11.3)	-10.5 to -5.5
2 to 4 units	48 (5.6)	136 (17.1)	-14.5 to -8.5
>4 units	31 (3.6)	101 (12.7)	-11.7 to -6.5
Acute kidney injury stage 2 or 3 — %	1.7	4.4	-4.4 to -1.0
Coronary-artery obstruction — %	0.2	0.0	-0.2 to 0.8
Major vascular complication — %	6.0	1.1	3.2 to 6.7
Cardiac perforation — %	1.7	0.9	-0.2 to 2.0
Cardiogenic shock — %	1.1	3.8	-4.2 to -1.1
Permanent pacemaker implantation — %	25.9	6.6	15.9 to 22.7
Atrial fibrillation — %	12.9	43.4	-34.7 to -26.4

* Values are estimated incidence (median of the posterior probability distribution, as calculated by means of Bayesian analysis), except for transfusion values, which are the numbers of patients and percentages. For all the values, 95% credible intervals were calculated for the difference between groups. Percentages may not total 100 because of rounding.

Figure 2 Components of the Table

The **legend** identifies the specific the topic or the point of the Table. The legend should be brief. The **column headings** consist of headings that identify the items listed in the columns below them, subheadings as necessary, and units of measurement as necessary. Column headings should be brief. The **body** contains the listing of individual items or data given (columns on the left) and the corresponding data (columns on the right). **Footnotes** are phrases or sentences placed below the body of the table that explain items in the title, column headings, or body of the table. The items explained are usually experimental methods, the meaning of abbreviations or symbols, and statistical information.

4. Cases of the Tables

Case 6

Case 6 is from the article titled "Five-Year Outcomes after Off-Pump or On-Pump Coronary-Artery Bypass Grafting" published on *The New England Journal of Medicine* (doi: 10.1056/NEJMoa1601564).

The NEW ENGLAND JOURNAL *of* MEDICINE

ORIGINAL ARTICLE

Five-Year Outcomes after Off-Pump or On-Pump Coronary-Artery Bypass Grafting

André Lamy, M.D., P.J. Devereaux, M.D., Ph.D., Dorairaj Prabhakaran, M.D., David P. Taggart, Ph.D., Shengshou Hu, M.D., Zbynek Straka, M.D., Leopoldo S. Piegas, M.D., Alvaro Avezum, M.D., Ahmet R. Akar, M.D., Fernando Lanas Zanetti, M.D., Anil R. Jain, M.D., Nicolas Noiseux, M.D., Chandrasekar Padmanabhan, M.D., Juan-Carlos Bahamondes, M.D., Richard J. Novick, M.D., Liang Tao, M.D., Pablo A. Olavegogeascoechea, M.D., Balram Airan, M.D., Toomas-Andres Sulling, M.D., Richard P. Whitlock, M.D., Yongning Ou, M.Sc., Peggy Gao, M.Sc., Shirley Pettit, R.N., and Salim Yusuf, D.Phil., for the CORONARY Investigators*

Table 1. Outcomes at 5 Years.

Outcome	Off-Pump Group (N=2375)	On-Pump Group (N=2377)	Hazard Ratio (95% CI)	P Value
Second coprimary outcome — no. (%)*	548 (23.1)	560 (23.6)	0.98 (0.87–1.10)	0.72
Death	346 (14.6)	322 (13.5)	1.08 (0.93–1.26)	0.30
Myocardial infarction	178 (7.5)	194 (8.2)	0.92 (0.75–1.13)	0.41
Stroke	55 (2.3)	66 (2.8)	0.83 (0.58–1.19)	0.32
New renal failure requiring dialysis	40 (1.7)	45 (1.9)	0.89 (0.58–1.37)	0.60
Repeat revascularization†	66 (2.8)	55 (2.3)	1.21 (0.85–1.73)	0.29
PCI	59 (2.5)	52 (2.2)	1.15 (0.79–1.66)	0.48
CABG	9 (0.4)	4 (0.2)	2.27 (0.70–7.38)	0.17
Nonprespecified outcomes — no. (%)				
Cardiovascular death‡	237 (10.0)	230 (9.7)	1.04 (0.87–1.24)	0.69
Repeat coronary angiography	125 (5.3)	114 (4.8)	1.11 (0.86–1.43)	0.43
Recurrent angina	41 (1.7)	39 (1.6)	1.05 (0.68–1.63)	0.81
Primary outcome in per-protocol population — no./total no. (%)§	487/2148 (22.7)	499/2182 (22.9)	0.99 (0.87–1.12)	0.86

* The second coprimary outcome was a composite of death, nonfatal stroke, nonfatal myocardial infarction, new renal failure requiring dialysis, and repeat revascularization (percutaneous coronary intervention [PCI] or coronary-artery bypass grafting [CABG]).
† Some patients had CABG and a PCI.
‡ All deaths in the first 30 days were considered to be cardiovascular deaths.
§ The per-protocol population included patients who underwent the randomly assigned procedure (i.e., without crossing over to the other procedure).

This table shows the following features:

1) The legend is brief and clear placed at the top (*Table 1. Outcomes at 5 Years*);

2) The column headings are brief and concise (*Outcome, Off-Pump Group, On-Pump Group, Hazard Ratio, P Value*);

3) Each type of information has its own column and its own column heading;

4) Sub-headings are used in the table body (*Second Coprimary Outcome, Non-prespecified Outcomes, Primary outcome in per-protocol population*);

5) The footnotes provide detailed explanation through the use of symbols "*" "†" "□" "§"to clarify the outcome details in the table;

6) Lines of demarcation are used to set legend, headers, data, and footnotes apart from one another.

Case 7

Case 7 is from the article titled "Effect of apalutamide on health-related quality of life in patients with non-metastatic castration-resistant prostate cancer: an analysis of the SPARTAN randomised, placebo-controlled, phase 3 trial" published on *The Lancet* (doi: 10.1016/S1470-2045 (18)30456-X).

Articles

Effect of apalutamide on health-related quality of life in patients with non-metastatic castration-resistant prostate cancer: an analysis of the SPARTAN randomised, placebo-controlled, phase 3 trial

Fred Saad, David Cella, Ethan Basch, Boris A Hadaschik, Paul N Mainwaring, Stéphane Oudard, Julie N Graff, Kelly McQuarrie, Susan Li, Stacie Hudgens, Joe Lawson, Angela Lopez-Gitlitz, Margaret K Yu, Matthew R Smith*, Eric J Small*

	Apalutamide			Placebo		
	Baseline (n=64)	Before symptomatic progressive disease (n=64)	After symptomatic progressive disease* (n=30)	Baseline (n=63)	Before symptomatic progressive disease (n=63)	After symptomatic progressive disease* (n=30)
FACT-P total	115·2 (2·5)	117·0 (2·4)	108·6 (3·7)	117·8 (2·0)	114·5 (2·2)	105·6 (4·3)
FACT-G total	84·4 (1·9)	84·2 (1·7)	78·6 (2·9)	85·2 (1·5)	82·6 (1·7)	75·3 (3·4)
Physical wellbeing	24·2 (0·5)	23·5 (0·4)	20·8 (0·8)	24·8 (0·4)	24·0 (1·0)	21·3 (1·0)†
Social wellbeing	22·1 (0·8)	21·9 (0·6)	22·9 (0·8)	21·3 (0·5)	20·4 (0·6)	20·8 (1·1)
Emotional wellbeing	18·2 (0·5)	19·0 (0·5)	17·4 (0·9)	18·5 (0·4)	18·9 (0·4)	18·2 (0·9)
Functional wellbeing	19·8 (0·7)	19·8 (0·7)	17·8 (1·1)	20·7 (0·6)	19·8 (0·6)	18·3 (1·0)
Prostate cancer subscale	31·3 (0·8)‡	32·8 (0·8)	30·0 (1·2)	32·6 (0·8)	32·3 (0·7)	30·3 (1·3)
Pain-related subscale	11·6 (0·4)	12·0 (0·4)	10·3 (0·7)	12·9 (0·4)	12·6 (0·4)	11·3 (0·8)

Data are group mean (SE). Data are from a cross-sectional analysis, showing the group mean of the available patient-reported outcome data at these timepoints. Patient-reported outcome data were not available for 13 patients at the time of symptomatic progression, because the symptomatic progression occurred after month 12 of the post-progression follow-up phase. FACT-P=Functional Assessment of Cancer Therapy-Prostate. FACT-G=Functional Assessment of Cancer Therapy-General. *Includes patients with and without subsequent approved treatment for metastatic castration-resistant prostate cancer. †n=29. ‡n=63.

***Table 3:* Group mean FACT-P total, FACT-G total, and FACT-P subscale scores in patients with symptomatic progressive disease**

This table shows the following features:

1) The legend is brief and clearly placed at the bottom (*Table 3: Group mean FACT-P total, and FACT-P subscale scores in patients with symptomatic progressive disease*). The legend can stand alone and be interpretable;

2) The columns are brief. Short terms or abbreviations in the column headings and subheadings are used;

3) The body is neatly organized with subtitles;

4) The footnotes provide further explanations to the data with the symbols of "*" "†" , to the definitions of abbreviations, and statistical details in the table and statistical differences in the data;

5) The lines of demarcation are used to set legend, headers, data, and footnotes apart from one another. The cells horizontally or vertically are not merged within a table, apart from when required in column headings.

Case 8

Case 8 is from the article titled "Effectiveness of a childhood obesity prevention programme delivered through schools, targeting 6 and 7 year olds: cluster randomised controlled trial (WAVES study)" published on the *British Medical Journal* (doi: 10.1136/bmj.j3984).

RESEARCH

OPEN ACCESS

Effectiveness of a childhood obesity prevention programme delivered through schools, targeting 6 and 7 year olds: cluster randomised controlled trial (WAVES study)

Peymane Adab,[1] Miranda J Pallan,[1] Emma R Lancashire,[1] Karla Hemming,[1] Emma Frew,[1] Tim Barrett,[2] Raj Bhopal,[3] Janet E Cade,[4] Alastair Canaway,[5] Joanne L Clarke,[1] Amanda Daley,[1] Jonathan J Deeks,[1] Joan L Duda,[6] Ulf Ekelund,[7,8] Paramjit Gill,[1] Tania Griffin,[1] Eleanor McGee,[9] Kiya Hurley,[1] James Martin,[1] Jayne Parry,[1] Sandra Passmore,[10] K K Cheng[1]

Table 4 | Adjusted differences for body mass index (BMI) z score between control and intervention groups at first, second, and third follow-up

Follow-up	No of participants (No in intervention arm)	Mean (SD) BMI z scores		Mean difference (95% CI), P value	
		Intervention arm*	Control arm†	Intervention v control (baseline adjusted)‡	Intervention v control (further adjusted)§
15 months	n=1197¶ (n=556) baseline adjusted; n=837¶ (n=393) further adjusted	0.34 (1.34)	0.23 (1.27)	−0.075 (−0.183 to 0.033), 0.18	−0.077 (−0.191 to 0.037), 0.19
30 months	n=1094¶ (n=505baseline adjusted; n=772¶ (n=359) further adjusted	0.42 (1.34)	0.31 (1.32)	−0.027 (−0.137 to 0.083), 0.63	−0.042 (−0.163 to 0.080), 0.50
39 months	n=467** (n=232baseline adjusted; n=345** (n=173) further adjusted	0.49 (1.37)	0.63 (1.22)	−0.204 (−0.396 to −0.013), 0.04; (99% CI −0.456 to 0.048)	−0.177 (−0.386 to 0.033), 0.03; (99% CI −0.386 to 0.033)

*Baseline, all participants 0.23 (1.24); baseline, group 1 school participants only 0.29 (1.24).
†Baseline, all participants 0.15 (1.20); baseline group 1 school participants only 0.28 (1.12).
‡Adjusted for baseline outcome.
§Adjusted for baseline outcome, baseline pupil level covariates: (sex, ethnicity, deprivation (index of multiple deprivation score for home postcode), 24 hour total energy intake, physical activity energy expenditure, and baseline school level covariates (size (number of pupils on roll), % school population South Asian, % school population black African-Caribbean, % free school meal eligibility).
¶Includes group 1 and group 2 school participants.
**Includes group 1 school participants only.

This table shows the following features:

1) The legend "*Table 4 | Adjusted differences for body mass index (BMI) z score between control and intervention groups at first, second, and third follow-up*" goes above the Table;

2) Columns are neatly organized through the use of subheadings [*Follow-up, No of participants (No in intervention arm), Mean (SD) BMI z scores, Mean difference (95% CI) P value*];

3) The footnotes provide all information related through the use of symbols of "*" "†" "§" "¶" to clarify experimental and statistical details in the table;

4) Lines of demarcation are used to set legend, headers, data, and footnotes apart from one another. Each explanation is provided with a separate line.

Case 9

Case 9 is from the article titled "Effect of Continuous Glucose Monitoring on Hypoglycemia in Older Adults with Type1 Diabetes: A Randomized Clinical Trial" published on *JAMA* (doi: 10.1001/jama.2020.6928).

Research

JAMA | Original Investigation

Effect of Continuous Glucose Monitoring on Hypoglycemia in Older Adults With Type 1 Diabetes
A Randomized Clinical Trial

Richard E. Pratley, MD; Lauren G. Kanapka, MSc; Michael R. Rickels, MD, MS; Andrew Ahmann, MD; Grazia Aleppo, MD; Roy Beck, MD, PhD; Anuj Bhargava, MD; Bruce W. Bode, MD; Anders Carlson, MD; Naomi S. Chaytor, PhD; D. Steven Fox, MD, MPhil; Robin Goland, MD; Irl B. Hirsch, MD; Davida Kruger, MD; Yogish C. Kudva, MD; Carol Levy, MD; Janet B. McGill, MD; Anne Peters, MD; Louis Philipson, MD, PhD; Athena Philis-Tsimikas, MD; Rodica Pop-Busui, MD, PhD; Viral N. Shah, MD; Michael Thompson, MD; Francesco Vendrame, MD; Alandra Verdejo, MPH; Ruth S. Weinstock, MD, PhD; Laura Young, MD, PhD; Kellee M. Miller, PhD, MPH; for the Wireless Innovation for Seniors With Diabetes Mellitus (WISDM) Study Group

Table 2. Glycemic Outcomes

Outcomes	Baseline CGM (n = 103)	Baseline Standard BGM (n = 100)	Follow-up (8, 16, and 26 wk pooled)[a] CGM (n = 102)	Follow-up (8, 16, and 26 wk pooled)[a] Standard BGM (n = 94)	Adjusted difference, CGM − standard BGM (95% CI)[b]	*P* value[b]
Primary outcome						
Time with glucose <70 mg/dL, %	5.1 (3.0-9.7)	4.7 (2.4-9.5)	2.7 (1.6-4.6)	4.9 (2.5-8.5)	−1.9 (−2.8 to −1.1)	<.001
Secondary continuous glucose monitoring outcomes						
Hours of CGM data, median (IQR)	324 (308-388)	327 (309-397)	473 (449-489)	465 (423-483)		
Hypoglycemia, median (IQR)						
Time with glucose <60 mg/dL, %	3.0 (1.5-5.5)	2.4 (1.1-5.9)	0.9 (0.5-1.9)	2.4 (0.8-5.1)	−1.4 (−2.0 to −0.8)	<.001
Time with glucose <54 mg/dL, %	1.9 (0.9-3.6)	1.5 (0.5-4.1)	0.5 (0.2-1.0)	1.6 (0.4-3.4)	−1.0 (−1.4 to −0.5)	<.001
Rate of hypoglycemia events per wk[c]	2.6 (1.5-3.9)	2.1 (0.9-4.1)	0.8 (0.3-2.2)	1.8 (0.7-4.0)	−0.9 (−1.3 to −0.5)	<.001
Time with glucose in range of 70-180 mg/dL, mean (SD), %	56 (13)	56 (14)	63 (13)	54 (14)	8.8 (6.0 to 11.5)	<.001
Glucose level, mean (SD), mg/dL	167 (29)	168 (31)	162 (23)	171 (30)	−7.7 (−13.1 to −2.4)	.005
Coefficient of variation, mean (SD), %[d]	41 (6)	42 (7)	37 (5)	42 (7)	−4.7 (−6.1 to −3.3)	<.001
Hyperglycemia						
Time with glucose >180 mg/dL, mean (SD), %	37 (16)	38 (17)	34 (14)	39 (16)	−5.8 (−8.8 to −2.8)	<.001
Time with glucose >250 mg/dL, mean (SD), %	10 (6-21)	13 (5-20)	9 (3-15)	13 (8-23)	−3.6 (−5.2 to −2.2)	<.001
Time with glucose >300 mg/dL, median (IQR), %	3.8 (1.5-8.5)	4.2 (1.3-9.4)	2.4 (0.6-5.2)	5.2 (2.2-9.4)	−1.7 (−2.5 to −0.9)	<.001
Secondary HbA_{1c} outcome						
HbA_{1c}, mean (SD), %[e]	7.6 (0.9) [n = 100]	7.5 (0.8) [n = 97]	7.2 (0.9) [n = 100]	7.4 (0.9) [n = 95]	−0.3 (−0.4 to −0.1)	<.001

Abbreviations: BGM, blood glucose monitoring; CGM, continuous glucose monitoring; HbA_{1c}, hemoglobin A_{1c}; IQR, interquartile range.

SI conversion: To convert glucose values to millimoles per liter, multiply by 0.0555.

[a] One participant in the CGM group and 6 participants in the standard BGM group were missing CGM data at follow-up. Missing data were handled using direct likelihood. Baseline data for these participants were included in the model.

[b] Outcomes were analyzed in a linear mixed-effects model that adjusted for baseline value of the outcome being assessed and clinical center as a random effect. The hypoglycemia metrics, time spent with glucose concentrations greater than 250 mg/dL and greater than 300 mg/dL, had skewed distributions and were modeled using a rank-based transformation. For these skewed outcomes, point estimates and confidence intervals for the treatment group difference were calculated using the technique described by Hodges and Lehmann.[28] *P* values and 95% confidence intervals for all secondary outcomes were adjusted for multiple comparisons to control the false-discovery rate.

[c] A CGM-measured hypoglycemia event was defined as 15 consecutive minutes with a sensor glucose value less than 54 mg/dL. The end of the hypoglycemia event was defined as a minimum of 15 consecutive minutes with a sensor glucose concentration greater than 70 mg/dL.[4]

[d] Coefficient of variation is defined as standard deviation divided by mean.

[e] Three participants in both groups were missing central laboratory HbA_{1c} data at baseline. Three participants in the CGM group and 5 participants in the standard BGM group were missing central laboratory HbA_{1c} data at 26 weeks. All participants had a least 1 central laboratory value and were included in the model for those time points. Missing data were handled using direct likelihood.

This table shows the following features:

1) The legend is brief and clearly placed on the left top in the table (*Table 2. Glycemic Outcomes*);

2) The column headings are subdivided into two or more categories and then subheadings are used for each category;

3) The letters of "a" "b" "c" "d" and "e" are used at the upper right corner of the column headings indicating further explanations are provided in the footnote;

4) The footnote provides explanation to the abbreviations in the table and SI conversion. It also explains the corresponding notes (a, b, c, d, e);

5) The lines of demarcation are used to set legend, headers, data, and footnotes apart from one another.

5. Key points

- Figures are suitable for presenting pronounced trends rather than static or exact numbers. Tables are used to organize data that is too detailed or complicated to be described adequately in the text.
- Figures generally have at least seven elements: figure number, figure caption/legend, data field, vertical scale, horizontal scale, labels and data. Tables mostly include four parts: the title, column headings, the body, and footnotes.
- Only important data in figures and tables need to be reported in the text.
- The format for figures and tables should be in accordance with the requirements of the specific publications.

Chapter Fifteen Special Considerations for Second Language Writers

One of the differences between writing and speaking is that a writer has time to consciously choose the better way to express an idea. A speaker does not have this time and must rely on unconscious, automatic knowledge, which is why a native speaker will sometimes have an advantage over a non-native speaker, if the ideas are being expressed orally. However, the non-native speakers should sometimes have an advantage over the native speaker when it comes to written communication; because educated, non-native speakers often have a better conscious knowledge of their 2nd language than the native speakers. Careful, intelligent editing is the key to a well-written manuscript, not the language skills of a native speaker.

Some grammatical but non-standard patterns used by non-native writers are similar to the foreign accent of a non-native speaker. Although a foreign accent may sometimes be mysterious and exciting to the ear, in academic writing, non-native patterns will shift the readers' focus away from the ideas being expressed and onto the language being used to express these ideas. Sometimes the origin of the problem is a language function that is accomplished in one way in English and in another way in the writer's native language. In addition, if this difference is pointed out, a dramatic improvement can take place. In the following, some of these common problems are listed, in no particular order.

1. Common Problems to avoid

(1) Nominalizations

Normally the function of verbs is to express action; however, it is possible to express the action in a noun phrase as the subject or object of a sentence. Moving the action from the verb to a noun phrase is called a nominalization. Although nominalizations are relatively common in scientific writing, they are even more common in the writing of non-native speakers. Verbs can be very complex structures to master, and nominalizations may be a coping method for 2nd language writers. Whatever the reason, overuse of nominalizations is a practice that should be avoided. The sentence in Example 1 expresses the action through a noun phrase in the subject position (an analysis). By moving the action to a passive voice verb the sentence can be easily revised (Example 2).

Example 1

An analysis was made on the sample.

Example 2

The sample was analyzed.

Nominalizations usually result in the use of a multipurpose or nonspecific verb. The frequent use of the following verbs may indicate an over reliance on nominalizations:

Made; happened; occurred; was seen; was observed; caused and produced

(2) Topic-Comment structure

Languages that do not require a subject, like Chinese, commonly use a Topic-Comment structure (Example 3) for presenting information. English grammar allows for this type of structure and it is sometimes used to emphasize certain elements of a sentence, but it is not a natural way to present information in English. Native speakers of English most often use a Subject-Predicate structure (Example 4) for presenting information. Unless special emphasis is required, a Topic-Comment structure should be avoided in scientific writing.

In Example 3 the topic, *reducing the harmful effects*, is first introduced in an adverbial phrase, followed by the main clause. This can be used in a special situation in which this topic is being contrasted with a previous topic; however, if no special situation exists, this sentence will seem out of place and should probably be changed to a Topic-Predicate structure (Example 4).

Example 3

As for reducing the harmful effects, it requires intense therapy involving a variety of methods.

Example 4

Reducing the harmful effects requires intense therapy involving a variety of methods.

A related problem is the overuse of the existential *there* as the subject of a sentence (Example 5). This pattern should be avoided whenever possible by making the topic of the sentence the subject of the sentence instead of using *there* as a subject (Example 6).

Example 5

There are many problems with the alternative method.

Example 6

The alternative method has many problems.

(3) Overused Forms

The following structures have specific functions and they should not be used unless they are fulfilling these specific functions.

and so on; etc.

And so on and *etc.* are accepted and useful expressions of the fact that the preceding list was not complete; however, they should not be used without a valid reason. In Example 7, the *and so on* implies that some other important causes that are relevant to the study have been left out. If so, they should be listed, if not, the *and so on* should be omitted. Removing the *and so on* does not imply that a complete list has been given, it implies that for the purpose of this explanation the list is complete (Example 8).

Example 7

Obesity can be caused by metabolism, lack of exercise, a poor diet and so on.

Example 8

Obesity can be caused by metabolism, lack of exercise and poor diet.

Another common but easily avoided mistake is to use the verb *include* to introduce a list that ends in *etc.* or *and so on* (Example 9). The verb *include* implies that the list that follows is incomplete; so adding *etc.* is redundant, the *etc.* should be omitted (Example 10).

Example 9

Incorrect

Conditions that may exacerbate the symptoms include diabetes, obesity etc.

Example 10

Conditions that may exacerbate the symptoms include diabetes and obesity.

Introductory phrases

(It is well known that…, We all know that..., At present…, In today's society…, Nowadays…)

Transition phrases, such as *It is known, It is unknown* and *To determine whether* ... function to introduce the change from one subtopic to another. Because of this, introductory phrases should be avoided if a transition is not taking place. In Example 11, *At present* implies that something is about to change, which is not the meaning the writer wishes to express. By removing this adverbial phrase, the meaning is simplified and at the same time clarified (Example 12).

Example 11

At present, the incidence of lung cancer is growing rapidly among women.

Example 12

The incidence of lung cancer is growing rapidly among women.

Respectively

Respectively can be a useful word at times. But like *etc.* it should be used sparingly and intelligently. In Example 13, unless it is important that the tests were given in this order and the writer is certain that this truly is the order that the tests were given, respectively should be omitted.

Example 13

The patients were tested for heart disease, diabetes and tuberculosis, respectively.

Example 14 could also be improved by eliminating the need for the *respectively*. Although it is true that *respectively* serves its intended function of expressing *in this order*, the example only contains two groups and two corresponding measurements; the writer should match the group with the measurement for ease of reading (Example 15). Unless the two lists are too long to be reasonably matched one by one, *respectively* should be avoided.

Example 14

The average resting heart rate for the experimental group and the control group were 75 and 72, *respectively*.

Example 15

The average resting heart rate was 75 for the experimental group and 72 for the control group.

2. Key points

- Nonstandard language patterns in writing will distract the reader away from the ideas being expressed.
- Avoid nominalizations, topic-comment structures and overused forms.

3. Revision Exercise

Direction: The following paragraph needs revision before being used.

As for afternoon naps, this study provides evidence that a 20-minute afternoon nap improves work efficiency in urban professionals. The evidence is that workers in our study who had a rest in a darkened room for 20 minutes during a mid-day break completed afternoon assignments more efficiently than those who used that time working and so on. Unexpectedly, it was also found that requests for sick leave decreased more in the professionals that rested for 20 minutes than in those that did not respectively. There is enough evidence from this study to lead us to recommend that whenever possible employers should provide space and time for employees to take a short nap during the workday.

Appendix

Appendix I Key to Revision Exercise

Chapter One

Before Revision

the operations of system 1 are fast automatic effortless associative and difficult to control or modify the operations of system 2 are slower serial effortful and deliberately controlled they are also relatively flexible and potentially rule-governed

After Revision

The operations of System 1 are fast, automatic, effortless, associative, and difficult to control or modify. The operations of System 2 are slower, serial, effortful, and deliberately controlled; they are also relatively flexible and potentially rule-governed.

Chapter Two

1) Do you think the following letter is appropriate for a doctor to give a patient's family member? If not, revise it.

Before Revision

The patient has presented with ascites and probable esophageal varices resulting from chronic hepatic failure. Diagnosis of the varices involves esophagogastroduodenoscopy; however, this could further exacerbate the condition by causing further hemorrhaging. The prognosis for this condition at this stage is not favorable. The patient should have begun treatment several years ago.

After Revision

Because of your father's liver disease, fluid has built up in his abdomen. It is also quite possible that the liver damage has resulted in internal bleed from dilated blood vessels in his stomach and esophagus. The only way to know for sure would be to place a tube with a camera into his stomach. But this procedure could actually cause further bleeding and involves some risk. Please understand that at its present stage this disease is very dangerous and your father may not recover.

2) Which of the following sentences do you think is not in agreement with academic style? Why?

① Children with no father as a role model will become criminals.

② Children with no father as a role model may become criminals.

③ Children with no father as a role model could become criminals.

The grammar of the first sentence is ok, but it is not possible to conclude that all children with no father as a role model will become criminals! Be careful when you are making assessments in this way. “Will” is 100% going to happen, so avoid using it to make generalizations about everybody/everything unless you know it is 100% true. There are other ways to make it less certain, e.g. “will possibly”.

The second and third sentence is in agreement with academic style.

3) Rewrite the following noun clusters to express their meanings more clearly.

Before Revision

① filament length variability

② a hospital employee relations improvement program

After Revision

① length variability of the filaments

variability of filament length

② a hospital employee relations improvement program

a program to improve relations among employees in hospital

4) Rewrite the following sentences to express their meanings more clearly and precisely.

Before Revision

① There were 41 hospitalizations, with similar numbers in the three day and five day treatments (18 and 23, respectively).

② Certain surgical procedures are known to be capable of inducing malignant tumors, although the ways in which this can happen have been classified as rare and very rare.

③ The effectiveness of mammographic screening for breast cancer depends on its ability to detect and to exclude the presence of breast cancer, measured as the sensitivity and specificity of mammography, respectively.

After Revision

① Forty-one patients were admitted to hospital, 18 from the three-day treatment group and 23 from the five-day group.

② Certain surgical procedures can induce malignant tumors, although rarely.

Classification of the different ways in which surgery causes tumors should follow in another sentence.

③ The effectiveness of mammography depends on how well it detects cancer (its sensitivity) and how well it excludes cancer (its specificity).

Chapter Three

1) The following sentence requires revision before being used in an academic text.

Before Revision

As for smoking, it has long been known that it has a function of causing respiratory disease.

After Revision

Smoking causes respiratory disease.

2) Analyze the following four sentences. Which one is the best example in the academic style? Illustrate your choice.

① We wish to suggest a structure for the salt of DNA that has novel features that are of considerable biological interest.

② We wish to suggest a structure for the salt of deoxyribose nucleic acid (DNA). It has novel features which are of considerable biological interest.

③ We wish to suggest a structure for the salt of deoxyribose nucleic acid (DNA). This configuration has novel features which are of considerable biological interest.

④ We wish to suggest a structure for the salt of deoxyribose nucleic acid (DNA). This structure has novel features which are of considerable biological interest.

Analysis:

Version ① is more clumsy and ambiguous: it is not clear now whether it is the suggested structure, or the salt of DNA itself, that has the novel features.

Version ② starts the second sentence with **it** and **Version** ③ starts the second sentence with **this configuration**. Neither device would have been as effective as repeating **structure**.

Version ④ is best. It displays the following features:

- It is direct.
  - ◆ "We wish to suggest..." It is not written like "*In this communication is made a suggestion...*"
- It comes straight to the point.
  - ◆ The writers could have started with a general statement about DNA: *Deoxyribose nucleic acid is a nucleotide that has been isolated from many species. We wish to suggest...* To write this would have reduced the impact of the message they want to convey.
- The writers make two simple statements in two short sentences. They are not afraid of using the same word, *structure*, twice.
- Every word is necessary: "*We wish to suggest a structure for the salt...*" not "*We propose a possible structural hypothesis concerning the salt....*" The writers even avoid *molecular structure*, there being no other type of structure to which they could be referring. And, while most writers would probably write "*We would like to...*", they use the elegant "*We wish to...*".
- Every word is the correct word, particularly *novel*. They write "*features which are of considerable biological interest*" not "*features associated with considerable biological interest*".

Chapter Four

Before Revision

Four hundred healthy, willing and age-matched participants were randomly and evenly divided into a facemask or a non-facemask group. The facemask group wore a cotton face mask throughout their public commute time and the non-facemask group wore no covering over their faces. At the end of 60 days, we compared the incidence of viral infections between the two groups.

After Revision

The incidence of viral infection was compared between two groups of daily public transit commuters. Four-hundred healthy, willing and age-matched participants were randomly and evenly divided into a facemask or a non-face mask group. The facemask group wore a cotton face mask throughout their public commute time and the non-face mask group wore no covering over their faces. At the end of 60 days, the incidence of viral infections was compared between the two groups.

Notes

1. A topic sentence that includes the message of the paragraph was added.

2. The point of view was made consistent by changing the subject of the last sentence from *we* to *the incidence* and by changing the sentence to passive voice.

Chapter Five

Before Revision

Bob:

I have to be a little late for our meeting tomorrow; maybe 30 to 45 minutes. Let me know if it will be a problem.

Tom

After Revision

Dear Professor Smith:

I am writing to ask permission to reschedule our 9: 00 meeting tomorrow. An unavoidable time conflict has come up which could cause me to be as much as one hour late. However, I would be able to meet any time tomorrow after 10: 00. Please let me know if this is acceptable.

Sincerely yours,

John Paul

Notes

1. The greeting has been changed from a given name to a title and family name.

2. The statement about the need to reschedule has been changed to a request.

3. The reason for the need to reschedule has been included.

4. Rather than merely stating that he would be late, the writer has asked the recipient to choose a suitable time.

5. The final sentence has been changed from asking whether the change is a problem, to asking whether the change is acceptable.

Chapter Six

Before Revision

Lifestyle choices are associated with obesity.

After Revision

Lifestyle choices influence obesity.

Or Lifestyle choices are influenced by obesity.

Chapter Seven

1) The following three titles each need revision before being used for the study described in Example 12.

Before Revision

① The Association between Exercise and Stroke Recurrence in First-time Stroke Patients.

② Decreased the Recurrence of Stroke through Exercise in First-time Stroke Patients.

③ Exercise Decreased the Recurrence of Stroke in 320 First-time Stroke Patients.

After Revision

① Effect of Exercise on Stroke Recurrence in First-time Stroke Patients

Notes

By changing *Association* to *Effect* the reader can now differentiated between the independent variable (exercise) and the dependent variable (stroke recurrence).

② Decreased Recurrence of Stroke through Exercise in First-time Stroke Patients

Notes

If a noun phrase has an article, the article must be the first word in the noun phrase. So in example one, the article *the* pushes the adjective *decreased* out of the noun phrase. This means that *decreased* is no longer able to modify the noun in the example. The revision solves this problem by removing the article.

③ Exercise Decreases Recurrence of Stroke in First-time Stroke Patients

Notes

Sentence 3 actually has two problems: the verb tense and the population. Sentence 3 merely describes the result of the study, rather than the cause/effect relationship that was discovered through the study. The revision uses present tense and an expanded population to solve these two problems.

2) Answers

① HIV-1 Neutralizing Antibodies Induced by Native-Like Envelope Trimers

It indicates the message.

② A Dose-Response Crossover Iodine Balance Study to Determine Iodine Requirements in Early Infancy1, 2

It indicates the topic.

③ Measuring the Quality of Outpatient Treatment for Schizophrenia

It indicates the topic.

④ Quantifying the Burden of Stillbirths Before 28 Weeks of Completed Gestational Age in High-Income Countries

It indicates the topic.

⑤ A Bivalent Virus-Like Particle Based Vaccine Induces A Balanced Antibody Response Against Both Enterovirus 71 and Norovirus in Mice

It indicates the message.

3) Answers

① Test results and clinical significance of the four serum markers in health persons and others suffering with chronic hepatitis

Every research paper should include the "Test results" part, so it can be omitted. The title did not make clear of "four serum markers", and more information should be added to define these serum markers. Therefore, we change it to "four serum markers of liver fibrosis". "health persons" has grammar error, and should be revised to "healthy persons". "others suffering with" is putting too much emotion into the title, which should be deleted. "Patients with chronic hepatitis" are the population the reader may interest, so we need to place it before "healthy persons". Therefore, the final revision for this title is:

Clinical significance of four serum markers of liver fibrosis in patients with chronic hepatitis and healthy persons

② A Systematic, Multinational, Large-Scale Analysis on Comprehensive Comparative

Effectiveness and Safety of First-Line Antihypertensive Drug Classes

The target readers maybe more interested on the topic of this study than the method, we can switch the emphasis by placing the topic at the beginning and putting the method as the subtitle. It can be revised as:

Comprehensive comparative effectiveness and safety of first-line antihypertensive drug classes: a systematic, multinational, large-scale analysis

③ A Study on Unstable Angina and Non-ST Segment Elevation Myocardial Infarction in Acute Coronary Syndrome

“a study on” can be omitted without changing the meaning of the title. So, it can be revised as:

Unstable angina and non-ST segment elevation myocardial infarction in acute coronary syndrome

④ Nerve growth factor and neuronal apoptosis after spinal cord injury in rats “Effect of” should be added to indicate the cause-and-effect relationship between independent variable “Nerve growth factor” and dependent variable neuronal apoptosis. Therefore, it can be revised as:

Effects of Nerve Growth Factor on the Neuronal Apoptosis After Spinal Cord Injury in Rats

⑤ Treatment of Acute Hepatic Failure by Liver Transplantation

“Treatment of” can be omitted without changing the meaning of the title. It can be revised as:

Liver Transplantation for Acute Hepatic Failure

⑥ An Analysis of 38 Cases on Clinical Diagnosis of Primary Ureteral Carcinoma

“Clinical diagnosis of primary ureteral carcinoma”is the most import part in this title, so it should be placed at the beginning. It can be revised as:

Clinical Diagnosis of Primary Ureteral Carcinoma: An Analysis of 38 Cases

⑦ Content of the paper: The research is about the prevalence of psychiatric disorders in adults. After comparing the data from rural and urban areas in China, you found the number in rural areas is much higher than that in the urban area.

Title: psychiatric disorders: rural and urban comparison

The title is not informative and complete, because it did not provide the sufficient information for readers to know what exactly the research is. The types of the psychiatric disorders, population, area and research results should be clarified. It can be revised as:

Prevalence of psychiatric disorders in adults is significantly higher in urban than in rural areas in China

⑧ Content of the paper: The research is about the meditation and nursing, and the researcher used quantitative study to find out how meditation makes nurses better communicators.

Title: How Mindful Nurses Make the Best Communicators

The title is not appropriate because the title partly describes the topic, but does not give any information about the method of the study—it could simply be a theoretical or opinion piece. It can be revised as:

Nurses on the Move: A Quantitative Report on How Meditation Can Improve Nurse Performance

This title begins with a catchy main title and is followed by a subtitle that gives information about the content and method of the study. The title can also be revised as a more formal one:

Benefits of Meditation for the Nursing Profession: A Quantitative Investigation

Chapter Eight

Before Revision

Drinking one to two cups of coffee per day can protect against some cardiovascular diseases. Can coffee restore Cognitive Function? To determine whether coffee can restore cognitive function in Alzheimer patients, a group of age and disease matched participants were divided into a study group and a control group, in which the study group was given 2 cups of coffee per day and the control group was given a coffee substitute consisting mainly of barley. Cognitive Function was tested before and after the study for comparison.

After Revision

It is known that drinking one to two cups of coffee per day can protect against some cardiovascular diseases. However, the effect of coffee on cognitive function is unknown. To determine whether coffee can restore cognitive function in Alzheimer patients, a group of age and disease matched participants were divided into a study group and a control group, in which the study group was given 2 cups of coffee per day and the control group was given a coffee substitute consisting mainly of barley. Cognitive function was tested before and after the study for comparison.

Keys

1. The introduction
2. Coffee
3. Cognitive function
4. Alzheimer patients

5. Capitalization problem, 'Cognitive Function' should be lower case.
6. However, the effect of coffee on cognitive function is unknown.
7. Use a signal phrase: It is known that…
8. The effect of coffee on the cognitive function in Alzheimer Patients

Chapter Nine

Before Revision

To determine whether contact with children increases self-awareness among elderly people, the incidence of age-related accidents in the home was compared between two groups of elderly men and women. Two hundred elderly men and women were chosen by matching age gender and cognitive function. They were then divided into two groups: group A had contact with children at least one hour per day, 6 days per week; group B had contact with children less than or equal to one hour per week. At the end of 1 year, data from the number of visits to emergency rooms or doctor's offices for treatment of accidents in the home was compared between the two groups. Any accidents related to the presence of children were factored out of the study results. No significant difference was found between the incidence of accidents in the home between the two groups.

After Revision

To determine whether contact with children increases self-awareness among elderly people, the incidence of age-related accidents in the home was compared between two groups of elderly men and women. Two hundred elderly men and women were chosen by matching age and cognitive function. They were then divided into two groups: group A had contact with children at least one hour per day, 6 days per week; group B had contact with children less than or equal to one hour per week. At the end of 1 year, data from the number of visits to emergency rooms or doctor's offices for treatment of accidents in the home were compared between the two groups. Any accidents related to the presence of children were factored out of the study results.

Keys

1. The methods and materials (Study Design)
2. Contact with children
3. Self-awareness
4. Elderly men and women
5. The last sentence (the result)
6. A comma is required after 'age' in sentence 2

7. At the end of 1 year, data from the number of visits to emergency rooms or doctor's offices for treatment of accidents in the home **were** compared between the two groups.

8. The effect of contact with children on self-awareness in elderly people

Chapter Ten

Before Revision

Nearsightedness was tested for a correlation with time spent reading a cellphone in 200 teenagers. Over the course of the 4-year study, nearsightedness increased significantly more in teenagers that spent 20 or more hours per week reading a cell phone compared with teenagers that spent less than 5 hours per week reading a cell phone, no significant difference was found between students that spent no time reading a cellphone and those that read a cellphone from 5 to 10 hours per week. Figure 2 shows the data for all groups tested.

After Revision

Near Nearsightedness correlated positively with time spent reading a cellphone in 200 teenagers. Over the course of the 4-year study nearsightedness increased significantly more in teenagers that spent 20 or more hours per week reading a cell phone than in teenagers that spent less than 5 hours per week reading a cell phone. No significant difference was found between sight in students that spent no time reading a cellphone and those that read a cellphone from 5 to 10 hours per week (Figure 2).

Keys

1. The results

2. Reading a cellphone

3. Nearsightedness

4. Nearsightedness correlated positively with time spent reading a cellphone in 200 teenagers.

5. Over the course of the 4-year study, nearsightedness increased significantly more in teenagers that spent 20 or more hours per week reading a cell phone than in teenagers that spent less than 5 hours per week reading a cell phone.

6. The sentence that begins "Over the course of..." is actually 2 sentences and should be punctuated and capitalized accordingly.

7. Cellphone use increases nearsightedness in teenagers

8. Omit it. Put the figure reference in parentheses after the results.

Chapter Eleven

Before Revision

In this study, we provide evidence that cell phone use was associated with brain tumor. In our ten-year study, we found that the incidence of brain tumor was significantly higher in 3,000 cell phone users than in the national average (Figure 1). In addition, the incidence of brain tumor was positively correlated to the amount of time spent speaking on a cell phone. Although we used statistical instruments to factor out the possibility that a third and unknown variable was the mechanism behind the association, we can not conclude that cell phone use is the cause of brain tumor. Further research is needed to provide this link.

After Revision

In this study, we provide evidence that cell phone use is associated with brain tumor. In our ten-year study we found that the incidence of brain tumor was significantly higher in 3,000 cell phone users than the national average average(Figure 1). In addition, the incidence of brain tumor was positively correlated to the amount of time spent speaking on a cell phone. Although we used statistical instruments to factor out the possibility that a third and unknown variable was the mechanism behind the association, we can not conclude that cell phone use is the cause of brain tumor. However, the strength of the association leads us to recommend the use of remote microphones and earphones to increase the distance between the brain and the source of radiation.

Keys

1. The discussion
2. Independent variable (s): Cell phone use
3. Dependent variable (s): Brain tumor
4. Population: Cell phone users
5. Revise the sentence that contains the research answer: (Verb Problem) In this study we provide evidence that cell phone use is associated with brain tumor.
6. Writing mechanics problem: Missing space before parenthesis
7. Write a topic/phrase title for this research: The relationship between cell phone use and brain tumor
8. Revise the faulty conclusion: Omit the last sentence and add a recommendation: However, the strength of the association leads us to recommend the use of remote microphones and earphones to increase the distance between the brain and the source of radiation.

Chapter Twelve

Before Revision

It is known that retirement can increase mortality in men, we hypothesized that retirement can increase mortality in professional women who have spent 30 or more years in the work force. To test this hypothesis, we compared the mortality rate between 200 women who remained in the work force past the age of retirement with 200 women who retired at the age of 65. We found that after adjusting for other health factors, the mortality rate was higher in the retired professionals. We speculate that the crucial variable leading to an increase in mortality is attachment to career, not gender. Retirement can increase mortality in professional women who have spent 30 or more years in the work force.

After Revision

It is known that retirement can increase mortality in men. We hypothesized that retirement can increase mortality in professional women who have spent 30 or more years in the work force. To test this hypothesis, we compared the mortality rate between 200 women who remained in the work force past the age of retirement with 200 women who retired at the age of 65. We found that after adjusting for other health factors, the mortality rate was higher in the retired professionals. The results indicate that retirement can increase mortality in professional women who have spent 30 or more years in the work force. We speculate that the crucial variable leading to an increase in mortality is attachment to career, not gender.

Keys

1. The abstract
2. Retirement
3. Mortality
4. Professional women who had spent 30 or more years in the work force
5. Reverse the order of the last two sentences in order to place the answer before the speculation
6. Increased mortality by retirement in professional women who have spent 30 or more years in the work force

Chapter Thirteen

Before Revision

Writers Name: T. Wakayama, A. C. Perry, M. Zuccotti, K. R. Johnson, K. R., R. Yanagimachi

Paper Name: Full-term development of mice from enucleated oocytes injected with cumulus cell nuclei

Journal Name: Nature

Year Published: 1998

Issue Number: 394

Page Numbers: 369–374

Writers Name: K. Takahashi, S. Yamanaka

Paper Name: Induction of pluripotent stem cells from mouse embryonic and adult fibroblast cultures by defined factors

Journal Name: Cell

Publication Year: 2006

Issue Number: 126

Page Numbers: 663–676

After Revision

Wakayama, T., Perry, A. C. Zuccotti, M., Johnson, K. R. & Yanagimachi, R. Full-term development of mice from enucleated oocytes injected with cumulus cell nuclei. *Nature* 394, 369–374 (1998).

Takahashi, K. & Yamanaka, S. Induction of pluripotent stem cells from mouse embryonic and adult fibroblast cultures by defined factors. *Cell* 126, 663–676 (2006).

Chapter Fifteen

Before Revision

As for afternoon naps, this study provides evidence that a 20-minute afternoon nap improves work efficiency in urban professionals. The evidence is that workers in our study who had a rest in a darkened room for 20 minutes during a mid-day break completed afternoon assignments more efficiently than those who used that time working and so on. Unexpectedly, it was also found that requests for sick leave decreased more in the professionals that rested for 20 minutes than in those that did not respectively. There is enough evidence from this study to lead us to recommend that whenever possible employers should provide space and time for employees to take a short nap during the workday.

After Revision

In this study, we provide evidence that a 20-minute afternoon nap improves work efficiency in urban professionals. The evidence is that workers in our study who rested in a darkened room for 20 minutes during a mid-day break completed afternoon assignments more efficiently than those who used that time working. Unexpectedly, it was also found that requests for sick leave decreased more in the professionals that rested for 20 minutes than in those that did not. The conclusions from this study lead us to recommend that whenever possible employers should provide space and time for employees to take a short nap during the workday.

Notes

1. The unnecessary topic marker 'As for afternoon naps' was omitted from sentence 1.
2. The nominalization 'had a rest' was revised to 'rested' in sentence 2.
3. The phrase 'and so on' was omitted from sentence 2.
4. The unnecessary 'respectively' was omitted from sentence 3.
5. Sentence 4 was revised to eliminate the need for the existential 'There' subject.

Appendix II Reference Articles

Chapter Seven

Case 1:

Messier SP, Mihalko SL, Legault C, et al. Effects of Intensive Diet and Exercise on Knee Joint Loads, Inflammation, and Clinical Outcomes among Overweight and Obese Adults with Knee Osteoarthritis: The IDEA Randomized Clinical Trial. *JAMA*. 2013 Sept 25; 310 (12): 1263-1273.

Case 2:

Parsons JK, Zahrieh D, Mohler JL, et al. Effect of a Behavioral Intervention to Increase Vegetable Consumption on Cancer Progression Among Men With Early-Stage Prostate Cancer: The MEAL Randomized Clinical Trial. *JAMA*. 2020 Jan 14; 323 (2): 140-148.

Case 3:

Aglipay M, Birken CS, Parkin PC, et al. Effect of High-Dose vs Standard-Dose Wintertime Vitamin D Supplementation on Viral Upper Respiratory Tract Infections in Young Healthy Children. *JAMA*. 2017 Jul 18; 318 (3): 245-254.

Case 4:

McDermott MM, Spring B, Berger JS, et al. Effect of a Home-Based Exercise Intervention of Wearable Technology and Telephone Coaching on Walking Performance in Peripheral Artery Disease: The HONORR and Randomized Clinical Trial. *JAMA*. 2018 Apr 24; 319 (16): 1665-1676.

Case 5:

Bjermer L, Bisgaard H, Bousquet J, et al. Montelukast and Fluticasone Compared with Salmeterol and Fluticasone in Protecting against Asthma Exacerbation in Adults: One Year, Double Blind, Randomised, Comparative Trial. *BMJ*. 2003 Oct 18; 327 (7420): 891.

Case 6:

Verstraete S, Verbruggen SC, Hordijk JA, et al. Long-term developmental effects of withholding parenteral nutrition for 1 week in the pediatric intensive care unit: a 2-year follow-up of the PEPaNIC international, randomized, controlled trial. *Lancet Respir Med.* 2019 Feb; 7 (2): 141-153.

Case 7:

Wentworth JM, Playfair J, Laurie C, et al. Multidisciplinary diabetes care with and without bariatric surgery in overweight people: a randomised controlled trial. *Lancet Diabetes Endocrinol.* 2014 Jul; 2 (7): 545-552.

Case 8:

Bangalore S, Maron DJ, O'Brien SM, et al. Management of Coronary Disease in Patients with Advanced Kidney Disease. *N Engl J Med.* 2020 Apr 23; 382 (17): 1608-1618.

Case 9:

Maron DJ, Hochman JS, Reynolds HR, et al. Research Group. Initial Invasive or Conservative Strategy for Stable Coronary Disease. *N Engl J Med.* 2020 Apr 9; 382 (15): 1395-1407.

Case 10:

Lindekilde N, Scheuer SH, Diaz LJ, et al. Risk of Developing Type 2 Diabetes in Individuals with a Psychiatric Disorder: A Nationwide Register-Based Cohort Study. *Diabetes Care.* 2022 Mar 1; 45 (3): 724-733.

Case 11:

Waalewijn H, Chan MK, Bollen PDJ, et al. Dolutegravir dosing for children with HIV weighing less than 20 kg: pharmacokinetic and safety substudies nested in the open-label, multicentre, randomised, non-inferiority ODYSSEY trial. *Lancet HIV.* 2022 May; 9 (5): e341-e352.

Case 12:

Ryan D, Price D, Musgrave SD, et al. Clinical and cost effectiveness of mobile phone supported self-monitoring of asthma: multicentre randomised controlled trial. *BMJ.* 2012 Mar 23; 344: e1756.

Case 13:

Pratley RE, Kanapka LG, Rickels MR, et al. Effect of Continuous Glucose Monitoring on Hypoglycemia in Older Adults With Type 1 Diabetes: A Randomized Clinical Trial. *JAMA.* 2020 Jun 16; 323 (23): 2397-2406.

Case 14:

Hershman DL, Unger JM, Greenlee H, et al. Effect of Acupuncture vs Sham Acupuncture or Waitlist Control on Joint Pain Related to Aromatase Inhibitors Among Women With Early-Stage Breast Cancer: A Randomized Clinical Trial. *JAMA.* 2018 Jul 10; 320 (2): 167-176.

Case 15:

Ahimastos AA, Walker PJ, Askew C, et al. Effect of Ramipril on Walking Times and Quality of Life among Patients with Peripheral Artery Disease and Intermittent Claudication: a Randomized Controlled Trial. *JAMA.* 2013 Feb 6; 309 (5): 453-460.

Case 16:

Yu J, Huang C, Sun Y, et al. Effect of Laparoscopic vs Open Distal Gastrectomy on 3-Year Disease-Free Survival in Patients With Locally Advanced Gastric Cancer: The CLASS-01 Randomized Clinical Trial. *JAMA.* 2019 May 28; 321 (20): 1983-1992.

Case 17:

Ravaud P, Flipo RM, Boutron I, et al. ARTIST (osteoarthritis intervention standardized) study of standardised consultation versus usual care for patients with osteoarthritis of the knee in primary care in France: pragmatic randomised controlled trial. *BMJ.* 2009 Feb 23; 338: b421.

Chapter Eight

Case 1:

Wentworth JM, Playfair J, Laurie C, et al. Multidisciplinary diabetes care with and without bariatric surgery in overweight people: a randomised controlled trial. *Lancet Diabetes Endocrinol.* 2014 Jul; 2 (7): 545-552.

Case 2:

Barbarawi M, Kheiri B, Zayed Y, et al. Vitamin D Supplementation and Cardiovascular Disease Risks in More Than 83 000 Individuals in 21 Randomized Clinical Trials: A Meta-analysis. *JAMA Cardiol.* 2019 Aug 1; 4 (8): 765-776.

Chapter Nine

Case 1:

Lee LY, Cazier JB, Angelis V, et al. COVID-19 mortality in patients with cancer on chemotherapy or other anticancer treatments: a prospective cohort study. *Lancet.* 2020 Jun 20; 395 (10241): 1919 -1926.

Case 2:

Kelly AS, Auerbach P, Barrientos-Perez M, et al. A Randomized, Controlled Trial of Liraglutide for Adolescents with Obesity. *N Engl J Med.* 2020 May; 382 (22): 2117-2128.

Chapter Ten

Case 1:

Yang J, Christophi CA, Farioli A, et al. Association Between Push-up Exercise Capacity and Future Cardiovascular Events Among Active Adult Men. *JAMA Netw Open.* 2019 Feb 1; 2 (2): e188341.

Case 2:

Hajek P, Phillips-Waller A, Przulj D, et al. A Randomized Trial of E-Cigarettes versus Nicotine-Replacement Therapy. *N Engl J Med.* 2019 Feb 14; 380 (7): 629-637.

Chapter Eleven

Case 1:

Chen H, Kwong JC, Copes R et al. Living near major roads and the incidence of dementia, Parkinson's disease, and multiple sclerosis: a population-based cohort study. *Lancet.* 2017 Feb 18; 389 (10070): 718-726.

Case 2:

Kurth T, Rist PM, Ridker PM, et al. Association of Migraine With Aura and Other Risk Factors With Incident Cardiovascular Disease in Women. *JAMA*. 2020 Jun 9; 323 (22): 2281-2289.

Chapter Twelve

Case 1:

Coupland CAC, Hill T, Dening T, et al. Anticholinergic Drug Exposure and the Risk of Dementia: A Nested Case-Control Study. *JAMA Intern Med.* 2019 Aug 1; 179 (8): 1084-1093.

Case 2:

Perkovic V, Jardine MJ, Neal B, et al. Canagliflozin and Renal Outcomes in Type 2 Diabetes and Nephropathy. *N Engl J Med.* 2019 Jun 13; 380 (24): 2295-2306.

Case 3:

Collaborative Group on Hormonal Factors in Breast Cancer. Type and timing of menopausal hormone therapy and breast cancer risk: individual participant meta-analysis of the worldwide epidemiological evidence. *Lancet.* 2019 Sep 28; 394 (10204): 1159-1168.

Chapter Fourteen

Case 1:

Blagev DP, Harris D, Dunn AC, et al. Clinical presentation, treatment, and short-term outcomes of lung injury associated with e-cigarettes or vaping: a prospective observational cohort study. *Lancet*. 2019 Dec 7; 394 (10214): 2073-2083.

Case 2:

Hajek P, Phillips-Waller A, Przulj D, et al. A Randomized Trial of E-Cigarettes versus Nicotine-Replacement Therapy. *N Engl J Med*. 2019 Feb 14; 380 (7): 629-637.

Case 3:

Jain N, Keating M, Thompson P, et al. Ibrutinib and Venetoclax for First-Line Treatment of CLL. *N Engl J Med*. 2019 May 30; 380 (22): 2095-2103.

Case 4:

Palmer T, Wallace L, Pollock KG, et al. Prevalence of cervical disease at age 20 after immunisation with bivalent HPV vaccine at age 12-13 in Scotland: retrospective population study. *BMJ*. 2019 Apr 3; 365: l1161.

Case 5:

da Silva Selistre L, Rech DL, de Souza V, et al. Diagnostic Performance of Creatinine-Based Equations for Estimating Glomerular Filtration Rate in Adults 65 Years and Older. *JAMA Intern Med*. 2019 Jun 1; 179 (6): 796-804.

Case 6:

Lamy AR, Devereaux PJ, Yusuf S. Five-Year Outcomes after Off-Pump or On-Pump Coronary-Artery Bypass Grafting. *N Engl J Med*. 2017 Mar 2; 376 (9): 894-895.

Case 7:

Saad F, Cella D, Basch E, et al. Effect of apalutamide on health-related quality of life in patients with non-metastatic castration-resistant prostate cancer: an analysis of the SPARTAN randomised, placebo-controlled, phase 3 trial. *Lancet Oncol*. 2018 Oct; 19 (10): 1404-1416.

Case 8:

Adab P, Pallan MJ, Lancashire ER, et al. Effectiveness of a childhood obesity prevention programme delivered through schools, targeting 6 and 7 year olds: cluster randomised controlled trial (WAVES study). *BMJ*. 2018 Feb 7; 360: k211.

Case 9:

Pratley RE, kanapka LG, Rickels MR, et al. Effect of Continuous Glucose Monitoring on Hypogly cemia in older Adults with Type 1 Diabetes: A Randomized Clinical Trial. *JAMA*. 2020 Jun 16; 323(23): 2397-2406.

Appendix III Bibliography

[1] Bahadoran Z, Mirmiran P, Zadeh-Vakili A, et al. The principles of biomedical scientific writing: results[J]. *Int J Endocrinol Metab*, 2019, 17 (2): e92113.

[2] Brian D. *International Standards for Students' Writing*[M]. Beijing: Tsinghua University Press, 2002.

[3] Day R.A. *How to Write and Publish a Scientific Paper? (4th ed.)*[M]. Phoenix: Oryx Press, 1998.

[4] Finegan E. *Language: Its structure and use*[M]. Boston: Thomson Wadsworth, 1999.

[5] Fiske A. P. *The four elementary forms of sociality: framework for a unified theory of social relations*[J]. Psychological Review, 1992, 99, 689-723.

[6] Gass M, Selinker L. *Second language acquisition*[M]. New York: Routledge, 2008.

[7] Gee J. P. The narrativization of experience in the oral style[J]. *Journal of Education*, 1985, 167(1): 9-35.

[8] International Committee of Medical Journal Editors (ICMJE). *International Committee of Medical Journal Editors (ICMJE) Recommendations for the Conduct, Reporting, Editing and Publication of Scholarly Work in Medical Journals: Sample References.*[OL] http://www.nlm.nih.gov/bsd/uniform_requirements.html [Accessed: 26 Jul. 2015].

[9] Kallestinova E. D. How to write your first research paper[J]. *Yale Journal of Biology and Medicine*, 2011, 84, 181-190.

[10] Martin R. R. *Get Published! Successful Scientific Writing*[M]. Beijing: Tsinghua University Press, 2015.

[11] Pears R., Shields G. *Cite Them Right: The Essential Referencing Guide (8th ed.)*[M]. London: Palgrave Macmillan, 2010.

[12] Strunk Jr.W. *The elements of style*[M]. New York: Dover, 2006.

[13] Strunk Jr.W., White, E. B. *The Element of Style (4th ed.)*[M]. London: Pearson Education, 2014.

[14] Swales M. J. *Genre Analysis: English in Academic Research Settings*[M]. Shanghai: Shanghai Foreign Language Education Press, 2001.
[15] Thurman S. *The Only Grammar Book You'll Ever Need*[M]. Massachusetts: Adams Media, 2003.
[16] University of Chicago. *The Chicago Manual of Style: The Essential Guide for Writers, Editors, and Publishers (16th ed.)*[M]. Chicago: The University of Chicago Press, 2010.
[17] Yule G. *Explaining English grammar*[M]. Oxford: Oxford University Press, 2000.
[18] Zeiger M. *Essentials of writing biomedical research papers*[M]. New York: McGraw Hill, 1991.
[19] 澳伟林，李玉林．生物医学英语写作与阅读 [M]．北京：人民卫生出版社，2008.
[20] 薄冰．高级英语语法 [M]．北京：高等教育出版社，1994.
[21] 程爱民，祁寿华．英语学术论文写作纲要 [M]. 上海：上海外语教育出版社，2005.
[22] 丁往道，吴冰，钟美荪，等．英语写作手册（第 2 版）[M]．北京：外语教学与研究出版社，2010.
[23] 蒂姆・斯科恩著，杨朝军译．科技英语写作指南（双语版）[M]．北京：科学出版社，2014.
[24] 葛传槼．葛传槼英语写作 [M]．上海：上海译文出版社，2013.
[25] 侯维瑞．英语语体 [M]．上海：上海外语教育出版社，1988.
[26] 胡壮麟．理论文体学 [M]．北京：外语教学与研究出版社，2000.
[27] 柯林・内维尔．学术引注规范指南（第 2 版）[M]．上海：上海教育出版社，2013.
[28] 拉姆齐・福勒，简・阿伦编著，田剪秋等译．李特－布朗英文写作手册（第 9 版）[M]．北京：北京大学出版社，2007.
[29] 劳里・G・柯斯兹纳，斯蒂芬・R・曼德尔．高级英语写作手册（第 8 版）[M]．北京：中国人民大学出版社，2008.
[30] 廖荣霞．英文 SCI 生物医学论文写作教程 [M]．北京：科学出版社，2012.
[31] 刘振海，刘永新，陈忠财，等．中英文科技论文写作教程 [M]．北京：高等教育出版社，2007.
[32] 罗伯特・A・戴，芭芭拉・盖斯特尔编著，顾良军等译．科技论文写作与发表教程（第 7 版）[M]．北京：中国协和医科大学出版社，2013.
[33] 玛格丽特・卡吉尔，帕特里克・奥康纳．如何写出高水平英文科技论文——策略与步骤 [M]．北京：化学工业出版社，2014.
[34] 任胜利．英语科技论文撰写与投稿（第 2 版）[M]．北京：科学出版社，2014.

[35] 斯旺编著，严维明等译. 牛津英语用法指南 [M]. 北京：外语教学与研究出版社，2010.
[36] 孙庆祥，唐伟，王申英. 实用医学英语写作 [M]. 上海：复旦大学出版社，2012.
[37] 王福彦. 医学 SCI 期刊论文的撰写与发表 [M]. 北京：科学出版社，2012.
[38] 王力. 中国语法理论 [M]. 济南：山东教育出版社，1984.
[39] 王佐良，丁往道. 英语文体学引论 [M]. 北京：外语教学与研究出版社，1987.
[40] 魏尔清. 生物医学论著的英文写作（第 2 版）[M]. 北京：科学出版社，2006.
[41] 文师吾，谢日华. SCI 医学英文论文的撰写与发表 [M]. 北京：人民卫生出版社，2012.
[42] 解景田，谢来华. SCI 攻略：生物医药科技论文的撰写与发表 (第 2 版)[M]. 北京：科学出版社，2015.
[43] 杨树隽，薛延民. 医学英语论文写作 [M]. 北京：人民军医出版社，2011.
[44] 张道真. 英语语法大全 [M]. 北京：首都师范大学出版社，2008.
[45] 张科宏. 说服 SCI 审稿人 [M]. 长沙：中南大学出版社，2015.
[46] 张俊东，杨亲正. SCI 论文写作和发表：You Can Do It[M]. 北京：化学工业出版社，2013.
[47] 章振邦. 新编英语语法（第 3 版）[M]. 上海：上海外语教育出版社，1997.
[48] 芝加哥大学编著，吴波等译. 芝加哥手册：写作、编辑和出版指南（第 16 版）[M]. 北京：高等教育出版社，2014.